# SYSTEMATIC PHILOSOPHY

# SYSTEMATIC PHILOSOPHY

*An Overview of Metaphysics Showing the Development from the Greeks to the Contemporaries with Specified Directions, Objections, and Projections*

**John E. Van Hook**

An Exposition-University Book

*Exposition Press Hicksville, New York*

First Edition



Library of Congress Catalog Card Number: 79-7362

ISBN 0-682-49398-8

Printed in the United States of America

# CONTENTS

SYSTEMATIC PHILOSOPHY

# INTRODUCTION

The subject is metaphysics; another way to name it, used here, is systematic philosophy. To some, metaphysics signifies what is mysterious, the occult. To others, it is what is obscure, unintelligible. In both cases metaphysics has some relation to philosophy, that is, the discipline concerned with fundamental, guiding principles. Joining the two views, metaphysics emerges as the body of fundamental guiding principles that are mystifying, esoteric, vague, incomprehensible, or perhaps even incapable of formulation.

Historically, in the tradition of Western philosophy, metaphysics starts with Plato and Aristotle in the Greek Classical Period. The chapters of this book are designed to provide not only a history of the highlights of metaphysical theory but more importantly an analysis of some of the great philosophical systems in Western thought and some critical commentary on the contributions of influential philosophers. The history, analysis, and criticism are a necessary background for the discussion of metaphysical problems. The intended outcome is acquaintance with the fundamental ideas and the working terminology of metaphysical theory in the tradition of Western thought.

It is not easy to identify what philosophers do or what philosophy is about. Many philosophers believe they write about great problems considered to be of first importance to the human race. The answers they give are sometimes formulated in elaborate intellectual systems. Metaphysics as a subdivision of philosophy treats the problems and systems dealing with the nature of "reality" or questions of "what is." It is distinguished from epistemology, or theory of knowledge, which considers questions about knowledge and what is known. Metaphysics differs also from logic, which concentrates on the formal laws of consecutive discourse. And finally, metaphysics is not value theory, which is on the one hand aesthetics, or theory of beauty, and on the other hand ethics, or theory of morality. Metaphysics develops systematic basic theory about the overall framework of reality with the details left aside. It responds to the impulse, the desire, to know and to know in general terms. If it is comprehensive, it develops thorough systematic answers to our central questions, using only natural human faculties, of which reason is the chief one. Metaphysics aspires to provide a comprehensive account of what there is, that is, the structure of all being; it analyzes the basic concepts that are used in describing the world.

The entire sweep of Western civilization from the Greeks of classical times up to our own day is the scope for this presentation. Kant's modest proposal to abandon the high aspiration of unlocking the universe's secrets and, instead, rest content with a revised program of depicting the structure of our thought about the world is an important transitional point. Questions raised will be those such as would be needed for a general account of the main features of the world. What categories do we need for understanding the world? What are the basic classifications of things? Are there any entities that are not things? What is a thing? Are there such things as events, or only objects which change? Are there properties as well as objects? Is there any more than a collection of qualities? What is a cause? What of space and time? How can one best get to know an answer to these questions? What is a good point of departure? What method can we use? Where does it all lead?

The questions are not modest, limited ones. One is not always sure of the questions or their formulation. It is possible to wonder if the answer delivered makes sense or even if it is directed to the question asked; does it overtax the limits of our abilities? In part, because of this, there have been and continue to be skeptical critics of metaphysics. They challenge the worth of the answers, even of the whole enterprise. Error proneness is a human trait; sometimes we are able to pick out the mistakes of others; we even catch ourselves making mistakes. Consequently, the need to challenge and revise applies both to the presentation of historical philosophers and to the analysis and criticism that are given in these pages.

An observation sometimes made is that the pretensions of metaphysics outstrip any likely performance. History shows a bewildering array of doctrines that causes a scandal of confusion. Philosophers have failed to arrive at agreed results. Courage, perhaps even rashness, is needed to write in an area about which there is so little agreement. These pages about metaphysics are in the first place descriptive, namely, expositional to explain what is held by different philosophers. Almost in the same sense they are historical and therefore cover a vast span of time. Finally, they are systematic in that they organize the data so as to show that there is direction and development throughout the course of the centuries. This is an overview, a perspective on the scope of metaphysics with some of its major issues, their key distinctions, and the technical terminology.

One difficulty with the subject of metaphysics is due to the various senses in which the word is applied. Sometimes "metaphysics" means the various issues considered, the questions and answers, the problems and solutions. This view of metaphysics is the most limited as regards the task to be accomplished. It deals with the specifics of metaphysical theories and in general proceeds by way of analysis. A second sense of "metaphysics" is discussion about the subject matter in general terms, its systems, the enterprise in broad terms. This view of metaphysics is more general. It is procedural, but not specifically about method, although method is part of it. Again, "metaphysics" as an activity critically considers the variety of answers and systems. In this way metaphysics is evaluative or critical. Whereas the first two views are mainly descriptive, the third is evaluative. Occasionally, some suggestions of a fourth sort, which is revisionary, are included. In this view "metaphysics" is constructive and attempts to build up a solid nucleus of the formal characteristics of any metaphysical system.

Another area of difficulty or source of misunderstanding about metaphysics is that there are too many theories. No one theory or system has universal acceptance, and most theories are internally consistent; yet, on the other hand, different theories sometimes disagree with each other. To make sense of this chaos it is still possible, however unlikely, to reach agreement by getting a theory which has universal acceptance. An alternative approach is to gather together the disparate points of view and sort them into some kind of preliminary groups or types. In part, this is what is being attempted here. We are attempting to develop a classification system. The possible advantages of a classification system are that it makes it much easier to remember and recognize large amounts of data, and, above all, it makes it easier to choose intelligently among alternative points of view.

The remaining part of this introduction makes and explains a proposal of a set of formal characteristics of a metaphysical system. Against this list it should be possible to check and challenge some of the major systems of Western philosophy and, consequently, to estimate their successes and problems. The proposal made in the introduction is developed throughout the course of the chapters. The design is to show that there is a direction, movement, progress in philosophy through the centuries. Not all systems of metaphysics are equally acceptable at any given time. As a Greek system from several centuries B.C. is unacceptable today, so also a contemporary view could be rejected by, but more probably would be unintelligible to, an ancient Greek. The sort of philosophy which is fundamental is metaphysical. It deals with existence, reality, or "what is," in the most general way. For this kind of philosophy there are some specific formal characteristics which say nothing about the content of a metaphysical system. Since the formal characteristics are a pattern or a model, the proposal being made is about the structure of any metaphysical system. The list with the proposed formal characteristics is given here and followed by a partial explanation:

Metaphysics is *systematic* philosophy insofar as the view is unified and the scope is total.

Metaphysics is *primary* philosophy to the extent that it is both basic and objective.

Metaphysics uses *reflexive* thinking.

Metaphysics gives attention to the *structure of language*.

Metaphysics along with the usual modes of logical arguments uses a distinctive kind of *presuppositional argumentation*.

Metaphysics is "systematic" philosophy when there is a group of ultimate principles or categories which are consistent with one another and applicable to all subject matters. The consistency or mutual support the principles give to each other provides unity in a system. Totality or comprehensiveness is achieved by a set of principles that are capable of explaining whatever is or may be. In addition to unity and totality, some hold that the group of principles must be final or stable, in the sense that the system is a system only when it is completed or finished, and nothing is to be added to the list.

There are objections to each of these characterizations of metaphysics as systematic. In fact, the whole idea of a system of philosophy has found many objectors in the later part of the twentieth century. Accordingly, the difficulties and objections must be regarded seriously. For example, some hold that the set of principles for a system must be the final set. It must be complete so that the list is closed and nothing more is to be added. But long experience has shown that development and progress do occur, and hence the list must remain open and cannot be considered finished. At best what is offered as a system of philosophy is to be regarded as a present formulation which can be surpassed. The elaboration of a system can say something about where it came from, how it stands now, and possibly the way in which developments are leading.

To be a system, metaphysics must be a total view; it must be comprehensive. In the spirit of understanding the previous objection to finality or finishedness, "totality" must be interpreted in the sense that nothing now known has been left out. It is comprehensive in the sense of "up to now" and cannot be taken as the last word with no new perspectives to be discovered. "Totality" is then understood so that the system includes everything discovered up to now but there may be additional viewpoints. Another objection to the claim of "totality" is that the scope of knowledge is so vast as to make it impossible for any one human person to incorporate everything into a single system. In a sense that is only too true. In philosophy, however, as in most area studies, one builds with and on what has been done by one's predecessors. Later efforts incorporate, reorganize, revise, and do all this realizing that one does not have to stand alone. In philosophy the writings of outstanding philosophers are the prime area of concentration. Working on the writing of others, the philosopher endeavors to comprehend, criticize, evaluate, and revise the work already accomplished.

A second way in which philosophy is systematic is by exhibiting "unity." Each part must fit harmoniously with at least many, if not all, the others. Unity is achieved not by the strong requirement that any one part be positively related to every other part but rather, negatively, by avoiding the clash of any one part with another. All major relations are to be established and identified. The requirement of unity, like the other characteristics, is understood with the provision that it is the best that can be achieved up to now. An openness to the future remains.

In addition to being "systematic," metaphysics is also "primary" philosophy. The operative word is "philosophy"; the modifier is "primary." The expression here extends not to all philosophy, but only to philosophy of a certain sort, namely that which is primary or first. Such philosophy is "first" in the logical sense, that is, the foundation or the ground on which all the rest of knowledge rests or is structured. It is not first in a personal sense of the most interesting, or even the most likely place to start, although it could be either of these. Further, metaphysics is primary in the sense of that to which one is led and which must most importantly be considered if the system is to be complete and coherent. Consequently, no unquestioned assumptions are allowed. Every premise, every principle, must be examined. In a figure of speech, the activity of primary philosophy requires us to lift ourselves by our bootstraps. We begin with problems, and only by analysis and comparison of various answers do we eventually reach a better understanding of the concepts used to express the original question. In the process we can enlighten ourselves or improve the concepts that we work with. For example, if we take a question such as "Why be rational?" the question is to be understood thoroughly before an answer is given. We must understand what it is to be "rational." Further, the question asks for reasons, and this asking for reasons is part of the process of being rational. Gradually, one learns that the question involves itself. And so one way to understand the question is to look for presuppositions and implicit starting points; the process of examining assumptions helps prepare the way to look at various ways the question can be answered. And so on.

Metaphysics as "primary" philosophy has in the first place the characteristic of being basic or fundamental. "Basic" is closest to a redundant sense of philosophy as a group of guiding principles. To use a ground or depth analogy, metaphysics is that sort of philosophy which expresses the underlying foundation affecting all that is built upon it. It is not that from which everything else is derived, but rather the base, and on the solidity of this base everything else rests. If the basics change, then the structure built upon it crumbles and collapses. Other than the depth analogy it is also possible to use a height analogy to elaborate the meaning of "basic." Metaphysics is then viewed as overarching. It brings organization by tying together all the parts.

In the second place metaphysics is "primary" philosophy because it is objective. In the strongest sense "objective" would mean metaphysics is the same for all peoples, in all places, at all times. Such a metaphysics would be never changing, never different; it would be accepted by all, rejected by none. History shows that though this may have been claimed by some, it has never been true of any philosophy, and hence there is little likelihood that it is possible in our day. A weaker sense of "objective" would be that in offering a system of metaphysics one claims that this is the best that can be done at this time considering the previous history. One may be able to do better, and the likelihood is that improvements will come about.

A different objection to the claim of the objectivity of metaphysics is that the theory or system of philosophy is related to the personality of the one who puts forward the theory. Hence, any metaphysics is subjective in the sense of being personal or private. But, granting the point of the objection that a metaphysical system may be real, close, or even personal to the one who assimilates and accepts it, one is still faced by the minimal requirement that a metaphysics be not only someone's view of the world but also a vision that will touch and enlarge others who understand and assimilate such a view. But "objective" as characterizing a metaphysical system must be more than that it is the construction of one person which may possibly affect others. Most who have offered metaphysical systems have made stronger claims to objectivity. To what extent a theory is the reflection of the individual author and to what extent it is valuable to others can best be judged in the case of each individual metaphysical system considered.

An important part of the proposal being made here about metaphysics is that it best proceeds by using "reflexive" thinking. Reflexivity is both self-inclusiveness and self-consistency. Self-inclusiveness is shown in part by the fact that questions about metaphysics are part of the study of metaphysics; there is no stepping outside the framework for a wider view. So, for example, the question, "What is metaphysics?" is a metaphysical question, whereas "What is chemistry?" is not a chemical question. A second and main way in which metaphysics is reflexive is that its principles, proposals, theories, etc., apply to the principles, proposals, and theories themselves. Specifically, each metaphysical system must be tested for internal consistency to put it positively, or self-contradiction to put it negatively. The consistency is not so much one of derivation as of the parts going together or not being antagonistic. It is the sense of "both . . . and" rather than the exclusiveness of "either . . . or, but not both." It involves a type of thinking which we may not do frequently but which we all can do. A help to understanding reflexive thinking might best start from looking at some negative examples, namely examples in which self-consistency does not occur. The claim of complete skepticism to the effect that nothing can be known with certainty is self-refuting. The claim cannot be consistently included within the total field to which skepticism refers. The skeptic's claim, making all parts explicit, is that "I most certainly know that nothing can be known with certainty." A similar analysis can be given to such phrases as "All generalizations are false." We find humorous a piece of paper with only the following words included within its borders: "Please disregard this notice." Perhaps some imaginative answers can be given to the following problem: When sign painters go on strike, what do they carry on the picket line? Contrast the above examples with the case of the leader of the gang declaring that the group just voted to give him a bigger share. When the gang protests that they did not hear anything about a vote, the leader responds, "Naturally; it was a secret ballot." Only those metaphysical theories that are free of self-negation and are internally coherent successfully claim to be consistent and self-referring. Metaphysics emphasizes that any claim or position must stand by its own proposal with thoroughness. It is, to use an analogy, like using a pair of spectacles to clear or extend our sight but at the same time being aware of the spectacles and the assistance or limitations they provide. Reflexive thinking carries out in a complete way the claim of unity, on the one hand, because each part is connected to every other, and the claim to totality, on the other hand, because everything is included and not even the system itself is excepted from the general requirements.

Connected to reflexive thinking is a mode of argumentation that is a sort of logic. Traditionally, it is said that all logical argumentation is deductive or inductive. It is claimed that all arguments proceed by way of derivation; the conclusions are a consequence of the premises. They are deductive or inductive depending on whether the conclusion follows from the premises totally and certainly or only partially and probably. While much of the argumentation in metaphysics can be classified under the above headings, not every one can be so characterized. Part of the proposal here about metaphysics is that it uses a mode of logical argumentation that is neither inductive nor deductive; it is "presuppositional," what is *pre*-supposed. Instead of looking solely to consequences, outcomes, or results, metaphysics looks to what is assumed, considered as a basis or a preliminary. Historically, the German philosopher Immanuel Kant developed what he technically called the "transcendental" method. This he spoke of as searching for the a priori possibilities of a concept. That is, given a concept one must discover the necessary preconditions of the possibility of such a concept. The intent of this mode of argumentation is that nothing is assumed or hidden; there are no unmentioned presuppositions. So, for example, subsequent thinkers look at the work of the philosophers who are their predecessors and discover foundations that are unseen, assumed, or presupposed. Consequently, they undo the work of their predecessors by undermining the foundations and must begin again anew. To the word "transcendental" Kant added "deduction," but that should cause no problem here. Such argumentation he called deductive because he considered that what he ended with came necessarily and completely from the starting point.

In the twentieth century there is a group of thinkers who combine the system of Thomas Aquinas with the method of Kant; they have been called Transcendental Thomists. Alternatively, G. E. Moore early in the twentieth century and much later John Austin spoke of the distinction of presupposition, entailment, and implication. The reflexive thinking and presuppositional argumentation as parts of the proposal being explained in this introduction touch on both the "transcendental" as explained by Kant and "presupposition" of Moore and Austin. In each of these matters, namely transcendental and presupposition, the distinctions made help to clarify the nature of the metaphysical enterprise. Since some hold that all arguments are deductive or inductive, namely by way of entailment, then an alternative sort of argument or logic, namely transcendental or presuppositional, must be established. Such has not yet been done. The basic approach explained and used here, however, is that before one can ask about the inductive or deductive consequences of a set of premises, such premises must be self-consistent and immune from self-contradiction.

The final point of the proposal listing the formal characteristics of a metaphysical system is the special involvement with "language." First of all, in a minimal sense, we are involved with language in the care with which we express ourselves. The accuracy and completeness of our words reveals the precision, or lack thereof, of our thinking. In a stronger sense, what is not expressed in words cannot be accorded the status of existing; it is to be treated as if it is not. In this view there is no opposition of thinking and saying; instead, the two coincide exactly. No claim can be made to thinking beyond expression. The claim to mental, unexpressed existences is set aside as unjustifiable. This view regards re-explanation and elaboration in language as the same as a rethinking or the expansion of thinking. The claim to mental entities that are unexpressed is useless, because we cannot do without language. It is our only expression, our only communication, our only check both on others and on ourselves. A third and even stronger sense of the mutual involvement of metaphysics and language is that we must look closely at the structures and restrictions of language. The elaboration of a metaphysical system must pay attention to how the mode of expression influences, and even may dictate, content. This point will be developed in various ways throughout the text. The strongest sense, but somewhat vague because it is in the developmental phase, is the tie between language and presuppositional argumentation. The search for presuppositions includes a look at the structure of the language we use.

The key formal characteristics of a metaphysics can be crystallized into a working definition. But first, a warning about how definitions can be unhelpful. The tendency is frequently present to read together "definition" and "definite." What is proposed here should not even be considered as an ideal to be aimed at or an ideal that may be achieved. At best, it can be taken as temporarily given, to be challenged, changed, revised, or even rejected. Consequently, the working definition is definite in the sense of committed. It is a target about which proof or disproof is to be developed.

> Metaphysics is the study of the fundamental presuppositions of some systems of primary philosophy.

The explanation of the key terms "primary," "system," and "presupposition" are in the senses already touched on. Though there is no explicit mention of "reflexive" and "language," these are understood as included in "presupposition," namely, the presuppositions in the structure of language.

Presupposition
Aquinas & Aristotle : Self evident.
Principle of Contradiction: Thing cannot be and not be at the same time & from the same point of view.

If you can't prove it, it's a supposition.

# I
# THE GREEKS

One unusual characteristic of metaphysics is that considerations about metaphysics are a part of the subject matter. Self-inclusiveness applies literally. The etymology of the name and the history of metaphysics are tied together. The tie is such that the etymology gives the early history and the early history is tied with the etymology of the name. Self-inclusiveness is accentuated when the history and etymology of the name both lead to a starting point with the Greeks of the fifth and fourth centuries B.C.

It is traditional to start consideration of systematic Western philosophy with the Greeks. Because this is the standard or usual beginning, to preserve this start may assist us in comprehending also the work of those who have made substantial contributions to further developments of metaphysics in later centuries. But the most compelling reason to start with the Greeks of the fifth and fourth centuries B.C. is the interconnection of the etymology and the history.

The first part of the claim made is that the etymology of the name "metaphysics" leads into the history. "Physics" is the root word of the name "metaphysics." For the Greek this meant nature in the sense conveyed by our word "physical," namely, the tangible, the perceptual. Whereas the word "physics" had for the Greek the additional sense of the natural as untouched or unchanged, for us of the twentieth century the experience of physical reality tends to be mainly of the artificial or the manufactured. The prefix "meta" joined to the word "physics" is the Greek for "after," in the sense of "above" or "beyond," or, to change the metaphor, "fundamental," "underlying." Taken together, "meta" "physics" has the sense of the study of that which is beyond or underlying the physical or natural.

The other part of the claim about the self-inclusiveness concerns the early history of metaphysics. As a name, "metaphysics" was first used not *by* but *about* some of Aristotle's writings. In the process of cataloging Aristotle's manuscripts after his death, Andronicus of Rhodes grouped the writings together under various classifications. One group had the title "physics." For us this would be more like parts of our philosophy of science. Another group was classified as "after" (meta) the physics. What started as a place designation, but not only that, has become a proper name: Metaphysics. The content of these works classified by Andronicus of Rhodes as "meta-physics" will be treated when we take up Aristotle and his philosophy. This first introduction to history and etymology is not to be interpreted as saying that the subject originates with Aristotle. We are saying only that the name originates about Aristotle. The names Aristotle gives to this subject-matter will be introduced later.

## PLATO

The history and the etymology do not give any detail or content of what, after Aristotle, came to be called metaphysics. A specific metaphysical view with content is that of Plato. He tells us a story and by way of this story helps us to realize a total world view. It matters little if this view is different from our own. If it is different, then so much the better. The contrast will enable us to compare the two and then have reasons for accepting or rejecting one or the other of the two alternatives.

The story that Plato tells us is about a cave with prisoners who are bound so that their sight is controlled and their mobility restricted. One of the prisoners who becomes free can look around and move about. He sees that the area of vision of the prisoners is restricted to a wall on which are cast shadows of objects. Movement of the shadows is brought about by objects paraded before a fire burning behind the bound prisoners. Beyond the fire there is an opening to the cave, and the liberated person upon leaving the cave and acclimating his eyes to brightness discovers that he can now see more clearly in the daylight, even "seeing" the sun as the source of daylight. Such a liberated person can now go back down into the cave and tell the others of wondrous new things. He might free them from their chains so they too can see and experience what they did not know. Of course, not all goes well for this newly liberated slave.

The mechanism of going out and coming back is important to the story, just as is being bound and confined on the one hand and being free on the other. There is a going up and a coming back down. The story is variously called an allegory because its meaning is conveyed symbolically, or a myth because it is created to explain important truths about life and its meaning. The puzzle at the center of the story is: "How do we know what we don't know?" The quick response is that we do not know and cannot know. But Plato, by the device of the myth, attempts to lead us to acknowledge what we do not know. We, the readers, are outside the scene of the story and oversee all that happens. We see the prisoners and their unfortunate existence. We learn of the one who is free and his personal triumph and social failure. If in our own experience we have been constricted for a time, we can empathize with the prisoners. If at some time we have learned something new, quite unexpectedly, then this may be a source of insight into the circumstances of the former prisoner who has suddenly and forcibly become free. To try to communicate something important to a group of people who do not know what we do can be frustrating in the attempt to communicate, but it can be disastrous if it hints at upsetting their most cherished beliefs. But Plato does not communicate with us in an important way until we will entertain the possibility that for all we claim to know and believe it may well be that we ourselves are like to the prisoners. It may well be that we have restricted sight and mobility and do not even know that we are so restricted.

So much for the story and a few comments on its mechanism. Philosophically, under the guise of the allegory, Plato is proposing a view that is total and is about the world, namely, the totality of what is real. He is proposing that the "real" is not what is immediately accessible to our sight, touch, and other senses in the everyday world of our ordinary existence. Rather, the wise man will understand what he sees and touches, and realize that there is an extraordinary and special reality that is in a sense secondary and derivative only because it is temporally later than average experience. This special reality is explained by Plato as a "form." These forms have among other things the characteristics of stability in the sense of unchangingness, certainty insofar as they are not vague or dubious, and they lack a temporal, ephemeral character. The forms ground, or back, or give foundation to all experience, whether that experience be of justice, or beauty, or goodness. We experience just acts, or beautiful things, or good deeds; but the grounding reason why some acts are "just" is the form "justice." The same is true for beauty and goodness. The form is different from but embedded in individual items of experience. The forms are already known by us and only because, for example, beauty is already known is it possible for us to identify some things as beautiful.

Given only this brief outline of a complex theory, we should still be able to look at some of the consequences that even Plato would have us notice. For example, education, in this view, cannot be an imparting or handing over of information or wisdom; at most it can be only a bringing out of what is already present to the one being educated. One who claims to give an education to another must therefore be in error. Again, if Plato's theory is right, it tells us about a way of life in the sense of where and how to attribute importance and attention. It is not individual experience, but rather the forms that are our true delight and to be valued over all else. Our life style should take this insight into account and assimilate it; then we should live accordingly.

The Allegory of the Cave gives us a view of life and living. A complement to this is the view of knowing in the "Divided Line." This latter passage is not so much a story as a set of instructions for geometric construction. Following the instructions, we end with a line divided in a proportion. The progression from smaller to larger represents levels of knowing, which are successive steps through which we pass. The first relation is that of images or shadows, which are secondary and derivative from concrete things. The second relation is where words fail us because this is where Plato is trying to bring us to acknowledge what previously we may have been unaware of and about which we are unknowing. Let us say that the second relation is that insight is secondary and derivative from wisdom. One further connection is that the first relation is mirrored in, or a shadow of, the second relation. Together, both relations form a proportion.

For the "Line" the lowest is shadow and the highest is form. But the same is true of the "Cave." This is a start to unravel the connections of the two passages which, though in separate books of the *Republic*, are successive parts of the whole treatise.

A more general way to put the point Plato is making in his philosophical theory is that he is apprising us of a distinction between appearance and reality. "Appearances" would be images, shadows, reflections, etc., all of which are secondary, derivative, and parasitic on something else. It is "reality" which is original, primary, and the source of all else. The use Plato makes of the distinction is to point out that what we regard as "real," namely everyday experience, is merely "appearance." We should "know" more, we should "live" differently. Plato proposes that we be wise and live our wisdom by regarding as appearance what many hold as most real; their values should be regarded as only a pale imitation or shadow of the basis, the ground, the exemplar, or the original of all that is.

An alternative way to approach Plato's metaphysics is by argumentation and the view of the world that comes from logical arguments. Parmenides is both the name of an historical person and the title of Plato's major dialogue on the doctrine of the forms. First we shall consider the person of Parmenides and some of his philosophical ideas, then consider Plato's dialogue of the same title.

Parmenides is sometimes referred to as the "father of metaphysics." The core of metaphysics for him is simple: being is, all else is not. The great division is between "what is" on the one hand and "what is not" on the other. The only thing that can be said about "what is" is "that it is" and about "what is not," "that it is not." This great division can never be reversed. About "what is" we cannot say "it is not," nor can we say "it is" about "what is not."

After setting up the foundational opposites Parmenides proceeds to explore the logical consequences to which this commits him. A first most startling conclusion is that no change is possible. The argument is somewhat as follows: What is, is—what is not, is not; but to change is for something to become what it is not. Since we have already said that "what is not" is not, there is no "what is not" for a thing "which is" to become. This might sound like word trickery or verbal sleight of hand; maybe it is, but a sketch might help clarify the point:

1. What is—what is not.
2. Change is movement from "what is" to "what is not."
3. But "what is not" is not.
4. Conclusion: there is no "what is not" for "what is" to become.
5. In other words, #4 means #2 is impossible.

A second equally startling conclusion concerns the evidence of our experience that changes occur. Parmenides adopts the position that appearances of change given in our experience are deceptive and cannot be important. We must be critical and use our reason and logic as a way to knowledge and understanding. The result is a "oneness" or monism in which everything is what it is and not something else. Its character is to be one, eternal, indivisible, motionless, boundless, and perfect.

Zeno, a disciple of Parmenides, maintains like his teacher that "nothing changes." Zeno attaches the negative "nothing changes" to Parmenides' thesis "all is one" and in vindication of his position has formulated some paradoxes of motion, one of which is the famous race of the tortoise and the hare in which it becomes impossible for the rabbit to catch the turtle.

Various strategies may be used to meet the argument of

Parmenides. One would be to reject completely what he is doing. This does not seem to be a legitimate response in philosophy because it is a refusal to deal with his argument. And so, granting that the argument has been made, an alternative could be to grant the argument but to qualify the consequences. This is an accurate way to describe Plato's encounter with the philosophy of Parmenides. Plato's framework is to divide as Parmenides does, but to admit both members. He attributes unequal status to them, however: on the one hand Plato admits experiences, changes, the individual, the temporal, the limited, but only as appearances, namely, the secondary and derivative; but, on the other hand, Plato admits as prime reality the forms, which are one, eternal, unchanging. The name given to Plato's solution is "Theory of Ideas" or "Doctrine of Forms." There is the really real, the forms or ideas, and then there is the derivatively real, the realm of sense and experience which gets its being and existence from the relation to or participation in the originals or forms. Changes in the world are not a deception, but a fact. Whatever changes, if it comes to be and passes away, is secondary and derivative. But the models, the patterns, the forms, or the ideas do not change. They forever maintain their unchanging, eternal, stable, and originative character.

How does this doctrine of the forms of Plato stand up? The first part of Plato's dialogue *Parmenides* gives a list of the major objections as proposed by the chief opponents, Zeno and Parmenides himself. To one way of analyzing the dialogue there are seven objections. They all employ the common technique that it is impossible for Plato's theory to be either of two contradictory alternatives. Since any theory must be one or the other and this theory can be neither, it must then be that the theory is untenable. For example, the sixth of the objections, and the one said by Parmenides to be the greatest of all, is that the forms must be known by us but cannot be known by us. The objection goes on to show that if one admits "forms," then he must claim that they are known to him or he cannot legitimately verbalize, much less prove, that the forms exist. But what is known to us exists in us according to our own sort of relative, imperfect, changing being and existence. Hence, the forms, having none of our characteristics, cannot be known by us or exist in us. The consequence is that the forms must be known by us but cannot be known by us. The general conclusion is that such a theory is untenable.

Whether or not this argument or any of the others is conclusive against Plato's theory is a matter for each of us to decide. At least we should be clear about the theory and its problems. The theory proposes a twoness of reality, one of which is more real than the other—a really real and a sensuous or experiential real. The point at which Plato's theory is most sensitive is in the relation of the two. Plato holds that one is original and the other derivative and secondary. Furthermore, the individual things of experience "participate" in the forms or ideas. What is this participation? Is it that the forms participate in the things? Or is it the other way around? Or both? It is unlikely that Plato was ever completely satisfied with any answer he attempted to give to this problem.

The basic problem is one that can be generalized so as not to be only Plato's problem but one that occurs in any theory of this type. It can be explained in the following way: If there are two sorts of things and they are to be related, then such a relation can be only by means of a third. But if this new third is neither of the previous two, then it (the third) must also be incorporated. But it (the third) can be incorporated only by means of something else (a fourth) which is outside all the others. And the problem repeats endlessly; an infinite series is generated. Another way of phrasing this argument is as follows: The intent is to incorporate two sorts of things by means of a third. But this must be done so that the third is not separate and distinct from the other two. If it is not separate, then it cannot do what it is intended to do, namely, to incorporate two separate sorts of things. If it is separate, then it also must as a separate element be incorporated; but this leads to an infinite series because to be included, the third needs a fourth, and the fourth needs a fifth, etc. The argument against Plato's theory has been given a special title: the Third Man Argument. It is as old as Aristotle and is looked on by many as the conclusive refutation not only of

Plato's theory but also the destruction of any theory that proposes to divide the world into two.

It might be claimed by some that it is possible for Plato to avoid the infinite series by simply staying with twoness or two types of things that are not related. Of course such a tactic would be self-defeating, because such a theory would not be a unified theory; and to present a total, coherent, unified world view is the point of the whole discussion.

In summary, the main purpose of a metaphysical theory is to present a unified theoretical general view of the world without such a view coming apart from within. If such a view is unified in the internal compatibility of all its elements, then we can call it logically coherent. The claim made here is that Plato's theory, or more generally any theory that attempts to make up the world of two elements, diverse yet related, is internally inconsistent. A way to show this logical inconsistency is the Third Man Argument, or more specifically to show how such a theory generates an infinite series.

At this point a few suggestions on the nature of metaphysics may be in order. According to our proposal in the Introduction, to be metaphysical is to give a general view. Such a view is general if it incorporates absolutely everything and excludes nothing. But such generality must have unity such that the parts fit together harmoniously and do not fall apart logically. We have claimed that it is because of lack of unity that Plato's metaphysics fails. Considerations on the characteristics for metaphysics of reflexiveness and presupposition will be passed over at this time; it is not that they cannot be applied to Plato's theory, but rather that they are not among the most clearly exemplified in what has been considered.

The characteristic of "argument," how it is both used and applied in metaphysics, is illustrated in what has been done so far. It is not enough to have a general view about the world; one must also be prepared to say why or give arguments for what one proposes. But arguments are formulated not only in defense of or attack on a general view; in addition, they can be constructed to show the defective structure of a view. This means that a view has unity or internal consistency only in the case that it is immune from attack that would destroy the view from within.

Finally, and this might not be so clear, what we have done so far has, it is hoped, made us aware of the care with which we are to use language. But, even more, it is the structure of language which has its importance for metaphysics. The argument Parmenides uses is a good example of how we are to look at and be aware of the structure of language. It was Parmenides who pointed out that we can adopt a viewpoint because it can be said and must reject a viewpoint because it cannot be said. The general point being exemplified is that the structure of language and the structure of a view of the world are importantly related.

## ARISTOTLE

The history of the word "metaphysics" has its earliest connection with Aristotle. Instead of starting with Aristotle we went back in time to Plato, his teacher, as a lead into Aristotle's metaphysics. Part of the reason for this procedure is that Aristotle's philosophy does not originate by itself and independently; rather it is related to and in some ways a reaction against previous philosophical ideas. The principal relationship is to Plato's way of viewing the world. The major difficulty with Plato's system as we have viewed it is the separation or "twoness" that it sets up. Aristotle's dissatisfaction with Plato's answer was the intrinsic difficulty that it failed to give the theoretical unity which was the reason for its formulation.

Aristotle proposed to remedy this defect by attempting to tie together the most fundamental and the most real on the one hand with the world in which we live and exist on the other. However, even to Aristotle it is not enough simply to take the everydayness of life and experience and equate this with the theoretical unity of a philosophy. Aristotle was too much of an intellectual Greek to take the individual transitoriness of experience for what is ultimate. Not every opinion or way of life is equally important and worthwhile. There must be a special quality to life and a special quality of experience before one can formulate the theoretical unity and totality needed in a metaphysics.

The moves Aristotle makes come off somewhat in the following way. He starts with sense experience, which he observes is in some way common to and connects the totality of what has life. But the individuality of diverse sense experiences is not sufficient. A link among experiences by memory allows such a living creature to convert past experiences to use. In this way the past can be valuable for inserting into and changing the character of what is happening now. And further, to be able to reflect on oneself and the world of experience is the mark of the living being that can understand and have wisdom. Such a creature, and Aristotle believes it to be true only of human living creatures, is able to have knowledge in the full sense of the term. The hallmark of such knowledge is knowing the "why" or the causes.

For Aristotle there are four causes. Each of these causes answers a different question "why" about a thing or state of affairs. If we can put together all four of the answers to these questions, that is all four causes, then we can be said to have knowledge. They are called material, formal, efficient, and final causes. They answer respectively the questions: What is it made of? What kind of thing is it? How did it come about? And for what purpose? Of the four, the one most likely to be understood by us in our time as a cause is the efficient cause or how something comes about, by what agency. Actually our use of the word "cause" most usually means only this sense of all the four Aristotelian causes. The one least likely to be understood by us or used in "casual" explanation is the material cause, or the stuff —what something is made of. It is only when "cause" is used so broadly as to cover whatever has a positive influence in something's production that we can even remotely comprehend using "cause" in this sense. The most controversial of the four is that of final cause, purpose, or teleology. But this use of cause is also the one which is most revealing of the special, unique character of Aristotle's thinking. Whatever our own view might be, it is necessary to keep final cause at the center of Aristotle's philosophy. Perhaps it is due to his biological interests that Aristotle makes so much of the notion of purpose. He holds that we cannot understand life without extensive application of this notion. Finally, the most difficult to understand of the four causes, and one most commonly rejected, is the formal cause, or essence, or kind of thing. The search for essences or hidden characteristics was most commonly rejected as useless and vain by the scientific revolution that took place at the time of the Renaissance. Be that as it may, the central doctrine of Aristotle's metaphysics is that of formal cause, essence, what a thing is, its being, or substance. Aristotle's general claim about the four causes is that all four are necessary for knowledge in the most important sense of the term. In the first book of the *Metaphysics* he analyzes the deficiencies of each of his predecessors as somehow related to their failure to incorporate all four of these causes.

Besides a special doctrine of knowing, Aristotle also has a special doctrine of existence, reality, or, as he calls it, a doctrine of being. This is properly his "metaphysics." It is true that the name metaphysics originates from an artificial cataloging of his works. But the name Aristotle gave to this study was "first philosophy." The basis for this title was that it alone was the most basic and fundamental; all other areas of study presupposed it, and it presupposed none of them. It was also the most general, all encompassing, with no details. Such a study is first not only in the order from the most general to the specific, but also and especially in the order of basic and fundamental to derived and dependent. Another Aristotelian name for this study was "theology," because as speculative and contemplative it not only called for the highest sort of activity humans were capable of, but also came closest to imitating the activity of the highest being, pure act, or God.

When all is said and done, names are extrinsic denominations. The content is more important. Aristotle puts this quite simply: this study is about being as being. The phrase "being as being" translates for us: being as such, being in general, being simply, and not specific kinds of being. This phrase is intended to convey the sense of the unrestricted and completely general character of the study.

A second important point to make about this study is that Aristotle, objecting to Plato's separation of the forms, believes that the "being" which he speaks of is not only part of, but the fundamental basis of the everyday world in which we live. The twofold criticism of Plato's basic doctrine of the forms is first of all that such a doctrine is superfluous and secondly that the split in reality by the doctrine of forms needs something else to repair what has been separated. Aristotle tries to develop a unified theory that does not need anything outside this world that we live in, whereas Plato's doctrine of the forms is superfluous because it introduces something more than what is needed for a general theoretical explanation of all that is. The second basic criticism is that the unity which is the intent of the separation of the forms from everydayness is frustrated by such a separation. The reason, as we have seen, is that the generation of an unending series frustrates the achievement of the initially intended unity.

Aristotle avoids these difficulties by locating "being," as the individual in nature, in the everyday world in which we live. Figuratively, some say that Aristotle brings the forms of Plato down from heaven into the things of this world. Positively, to emphasize the connection, or negatively, to avoid the separation, Aristotle identifies the principal meaning of being with that of substance. Though there are various senses of "being," not all of them are equally relevant for metaphysics. Aristotle lines up the following. First, there is "being" in an accidental sense. By this Aristotle appears to mean that we treat as real and actual various properties and characteristics. For example, "Black is the color of the ink on this page." Reality or being is attributed to "black." But this cannot be one of the more important senses of being, because the black which is real is always the characteristic or accident of some thing, in this case, the ink on the page.

Then, there is the "being" of the categories. The categories here are classes or types of reality. In the first place there is substance, or what a thing is, and then there are all those other characteristics of substance, called accidents. This sense of being is in the first place the primary category of substance, or that on which all else depends and to which all other things are related. It is this meaning of being as substance that Aristotle takes as the most important one for metaphysics, and it is the further analysis of the causes and principles of substance that is the main task of metaphysics.

An understanding of how Aristotle arrives at the list of categories that go to make up this second sense of "being" might be instructive. He starts from statements in language that can be made. A first convenient grouping of the sorts of statements is into those which have words said about them and those which are said about other things. The first he calls substance; the latter are accidents. Substance, reached by an analysis of actual language usage, is that which has predicates, that is, things are said about it, but it is never a predicate, that is, it is never said about anything. Accidents are always predicated about other things. Accidents get subdivided into various typical ways of talking about substances, such as, What kind of? How much? When? Where? etc. From the distinction of substance and accidents which comes from an analysis of language, he moves to substance, or what a thing is, as the fundamental reality or the primary sense of "being." Accidents, or the characteristics of things, are always secondary and related to something else. Substance, or "what a thing is," is the only thing that exists in itself. Accidents never exist by themselves, but always in something else. Aristotle's argument is that since language is about the world, then we can go from our ways of talking about the world to insight into the structure of the world.

The third sense of "being" is that of the "true." Here Aristotle seems to have in mind a definition of truth and falsity (*Metaphysics*, Gamma [IV], §7). Truth is had when we say "is" to "what is" and "is not" to "what is not." The basic idea seems to be that true sentences match what is or is not the case, whereas the false ones do not. Understood in this way, truth is not a prime sense of being but always derived or secondary, because it is dependent on an independent real state of affairs in the world.

The final sense of "being" is that of the potential and the actual. Potential here is understood as that which can be or is about to be but is not yet. The actual is always by previous analysis either substance or accidents. Joining the two, the potential is always related to the now actual or about to be actual. The actual is already included under the second sense of being and the categories. Consequently, this final sense cannot be the most relevant sense of being for metaphysics.

The general conclusion to this analysis of the various senses of "being" is that they all coalesce in or are related to being as substance. It is, therefore, about substance that the metaphysician strives to know. Moreover, to know means to analyze by way of the causes. In addition, the principal sense of cause is that of formal cause. Consequently, the investigation of substance and the investigation of formal cause conjoin to be the central inquiry in Aristotle's metaphysics. In a little more detail the argument is as follows: The extrinsic causes of agent and purpose, though important, when asked about being or substance are not the main metaphysical questions. The intrinsic causes, the matter or stuff, and the essence or structure, turn out to be the primary investigations about substance. The reason for this is that being, or substance, is the most general of all notions; there are no extrinsic causes, and there is nothing else, which is outside of this the most general of all concepts. Of the intrinsic causes, matter or the stuff of which something is made is certainly a prime candidate. Moreover, if bodies, or realities which are sensible, are not what substance is, then what else could substance be? It is perhaps quite difficult for us to understand that for Aristotle the sensible is not the basic understanding of substance. He argues somewhat in the following way: "Substratum," introduced as a new name for substance, is that of which everything else is predicated and which is predicated of nothing else. It is more accurately known from looking at the structure of our language than from looking at the world around us. Furthermore, this substratum could be in the first place matter, secondly, shape or pattern, or finally, a combination of the two. But substance/substratum as that which underlies a thing cannot be matter. The telling reasons against matter or stuff of which something is made is that this matter can be this thing or that thing, and this thing can be of this matter or that matter. For example, this wood can be a table or a door, or this table can be of wood or of stone. Nor can substance/substratum be the compound, because the form, that is the shape or pattern, is prior to the matter; and if it is prior to the matter, then it is all the more prior to the compound. Finally, it is only the form or formal cause which makes a being to be what it is and not something else. It is, therefore, form or formal cause which conjoins both the underlying foundation of all things and the predication characteristic from which Aristotle takes his initial conception of substance.

Besides analyzing substance by way of the four causes to develop our knowledge of the nature of reality, Aristotle also insists we are to know the principles of substance. "Principle" is used here not so much as the source but rather the governing rule which must be embedded in our treatment of the subject and cannot be violated without our falling into inconsistency. Aristotle believes he must find the most certain principle which is the best known and about which no mistake can be made. The principle is: The same attribute cannot at the same time belong and not belong to the same subject and in the same respect. It is variously called a "law," a "principle," "of contradiction," "of non-contradiction." The sense of it is that even were all else uncertain or denied, this must remain both certain and undeniable. It is in this way ultimate. He also calls it a starting point, but it is unclear in what way it is a starting point. He does not believe that it is a first from which all else is deducible. He could, however, be treating it as the basic presupposition which cannot be omitted, denied, or disregarded. This view is consistent with his further discussion wherein he shows any denial of this principle is fatal to such a system that attempts to incorporate such a denial. Though the phrasing of the principle leaves it unclear as to whether it is a law of language, a law of being, or both, the position of the treatment of the principle indicates that Aristotle regards it principally as a law of being and also a law of language.

There are other major doctrines in Aristotle's metaphysics. In addition, further exposition is needed to clarify the parts that have been treated. But, it is hoped, there has been enough given and explained about Aristotle's metaphysics to contrast it with Plato's system both by way of showing the lines of continuity and the differences of opinion and argumentation. The continuity is more in the sorts of problems that are the focus of attention, and the differences are more in the answers that are given.

Subsequent philosophers frequently worked from the fundamental notions in Aristotle's system either by way of further development, qualification, or denial. With Aristotle we find the beginning of a technical vocabulary for metaphysics. Later philosophers have added many of their own terms or revised those used by predecessors, but it is with Aristotle above all that we find the beginnings of key terms such as "being," "substance," "cause," "essence." One of the books of the *Metaphysics* (Delta, IV) is a lexicon of special terms. Consequently, some training in the terminology, distinctions, and arguments is needed to proceed further into the history and development of metaphysics. We have already started on that path.

Aristotle's metaphysics is in some senses an unfinished work, and as such it invites contributions from all who attempt to work their way through it. Moreover, there are other sections of Aristotle's writings that are not incorporated into the metaphysics. An indication of some remaining questions will help emphasize both of these sorts of incompleteness.

A first problem area is that of "form." The conception of form is central in the philosophy of Aristotle as it was with Plato. We might expect to find similarities between the two, especially since Plato was Aristotle's teacher. "Form" is the source of some of the major obscurities, difficulties, and objections in the case of Plato. In Aristotle's philosophy, "form" is both formal cause and a correlative with matter which results in the concrete individual thing. The conception of form which is so different in Aristotle's philosophy is equally obscure and the source of difficulties and objections. Form is universal; it is unchanging in itself. Things change insofar as new forms supersede previous departing forms. It is the source of intelligibility, in terms of which the individual existing thing is understood. But with Aristotle, forms are not separable from but exist only in objects of the physical world. But what is this form? It is structure, it is pattern, it is shape—all understood in an intrinsic, basic way. But there is not much more that Aristotle tells us about it.

An allied difficulty is the status of the individual thing. It is possible to distinguish Aristotle's philosophy from that of Plato by Aristotle's stress that primary reality is in the individual things of our everyday life and world. Yet knowledge, for Aristotle—where it is complete and thorough—is in understanding "form," which is not, oddly enough, the source of individuality and uniqueness. It is matter, the correlative notion with form, that together with form makes the individual thing. Yet matter as such is unknowable. Knowledge is possible only when form is joined with matter. For Aristotle, the prime reality which is the individual thing is knowable only by the form which makes it universal. The worry is that the individual thing which is the prime reality is not knowable in its individuality. Hence, the attempt in the system of Aristotle to achieve supremacy over his predecessor does not furnish a means of knowledge by which the system can achieve what it claims as one of its chief advantages.

A third sort of difficulty with form arises because Aristotle conceives nature in static terms. Each thing is what it is, and though it can become different, the difference occurs only when a given form is succeeded by another. There is no room for development and a dynamic evolutionary conception of nature.

A related problem area is that of final cause or purpose. It has been treated only in passing as one of the four causes, and this is certainly not an indication of how central teleology is in Aristotle's system of philosophy. For him, purposiveness is characteristic of all things, even physical nature. He does not understand "purpose" as the unfolding of a divine plan, which would be incompatible with his theory that the sole activity of God is self-knowledge. Rather, "purpose" is understood as nature's unconscious striving toward an end. For example, heavy objects fall because their natural place is at the center of the world, and they in falling when unsupported are striving to regain their lost natural place. But such a conception both of natural place and of unconscious teleology is unacceptable. Actions that are not random have results that are aimed at or imagined. But unconscious purposiveness excludes aim, imagination, or preknown results. Consequently, it is not purpose at all. Here the criticism is that purpose or final cause is an unclearly worked out notion in Aristotle.

A very general difficulty with Aristotle's way of doing philosophy is that it is a third person approach to both the world and human beings. Everything is treated from without, or as an object. There is no room for a first person or personalized philosophy. Humans are just another sort of substance.

Finally, it is only honest to Aristotle to point out that in his own view of his philosophy the conceptions of matter and form on the one hand and potency and act on the other have a far more central position than the treatment here has indicated. Their noninclusion has not been because they are unimportant.

# II
# THE MEDIEVALS

A chapter for the Medievals separate from the Greeks is in part deceptive. Though there are differences, it is nonetheless possible to regard both as a part of classical philosophy. They share similarities and differences, and it is the similarities that predominate. Such similarities are to be found both in the problems considered and in the direction of the solutions offered. The same thought forms and the deeper structures of the way of regarding the world prevail. The world is viewed as separate from humans, and the task of philosophy is to set out this structure which is objective and the same for all. Things have essences or natures which are not the surface, accidental, or sense characteristics. Nature is goal oriented and to be regarded as achieving ends. Viewpoints like these are the basis of the statement that there is a classical philosophy and that, for the greater part, it is shared by the Greeks and the Medievals. The differences of the Medievals from the Greeks will be more manifest in the course of the chapter. More extensive treatment will be given to the differences than to the similarities.

To understand Medieval philosophy some consideration must be given to Christianity. This is because of the impact that Christianity has had on Western culture and civilization, and because of the reciprocal impact that Christianity has had on philosophy and philosophy on Christianity. This reciprocal impact occurs mainly by way of theology, and it can be described in various ways. In simplest terms, theology took part of its conceptual framework from philosophy and molded key concepts to its own uses and purposes. These same key concepts came back transformed and, as transformed, worked their way into philosophy. This chapter in part will show how this happened, particularly with the key concepts of "world," "God," "person," and "being."

So far mention has been made of similarities, differences, and transformations by way of active interrelation; this sounds harmonious. But it was not so in the early days. Christianity was opposed to philosophy and what it stood for in its most general aspects, that is, as a total world view. The reason is that a Christian believing in a revealed religion could not accept something other than revelation as giving the total picture. Revelation in Christianity means that humans now have open to them both a way of knowledge and a way of life that are not known without this revelation. What becomes known to a human by revelation, while not necessarily opposed to, must be at least in addition to whatever is known without such an aid. If something more is known by revelation, then Christianity cannot hold that philosophy or any of its parts can be a total world view. Consequently, in its earliest ages Christianity stood in opposition to philosophy. Such opposition was not always to what was in philosophy, but to the claim that it was total, complete, and self-sufficient.

In his first letter to the Corinthians, Paul of Tarsus speaks of the message, or good news, of Christianity as salvation. This message of salvation is about the cross and the crucifixion of Jesus. It is foolish or illogical to human wisdom. Here, Paul identifies human wisdom with the Greeks and philosophy. He also writes that a crucified Christ is an obstacle to the miracle-seeking Jews. In this letter, Paul is in the first instance diagramming a triangle of opposition between followers of Jesus, the Greeks, and the Jews. But he also speaks of God's wisdom and God's power. The opposition is softened by the declaration that salvation is offered to all, Jew and Greek alike. All are called to a higher wisdom and a higher power which, at first, appears as foolishness and weakness. In the last analysis Paul is opposing current answers and systems of thought that propose to deliver total answers and a way of life. He is not denying, but rather declaring that Christianity has its own total view of the world and the place of humans in it.

The use of argumentation to establish a point is a distinctive characteristic of philosophy; it does not have the same principal place or emphasis in biblical texts. Paul's mode of thought and that of the biblical record of the words of Jesus is that of proclamation rather than argumentation. The message is preached and declared. Over and over Jesus contrasts, "You have heard . . ." with, "But I say this to you. . . ." The acceptance of the gospel is due to faith which does "not depend on human philosophy but on the power of God." Only several centuries after its foundation, when a theology started to develop, Christianity began to make extensive use of Greek philosophical concepts and logical argumentation to explain and prove its doctrines. This development occurred especially during the trinitarian controversies of the third and fourth centuries.

In the initial opposition between Christianity and philosophy there is a certain irony. Christianity, even though it rejects philosophy, is a viewpoint that claims to be total and basic. In these characteristics it is the same as philosophy. Though it may reject specific viewpoints, it is not exempt from being a general viewpoint itself. This is a good example, in part, for why it is important to keep working with the characteristics of a metaphysical system—in this case, those of totality and basicness. In addition, the practice of reflexive thinking will enable us to develop this insight. The practice consists in being able to apply what is being said not only to what is being talked about, but also to itself. In this case, to reject a total basic world-view is itself a total basic world-view. Though the specifics might be rejected, yet the general formal characteristics are the same. The phrase, "Philosophy always buries its undertakers," recognizes and sums up the irony about philosophy and its seeming opponents. The old pun has it: "Don't knock the undertaker, he's the last one to let you down." Gilson, who penned the phrase about philosophy and its undertakers, is reminding us that those in history who have at times proclaimed the end of philosophy, or even have claimed to tuck it away in oblivion, have been shown to be wrong. In their rejection they became part of what they thought they were rejecting.

In time Christianity became an influence on several key philosophical concepts. The influence was by way of opposition and transformation. A first notable opposition was between the Greek view of the world as eternal, that is, of matter as self-sustaining, and the view which is both Hebrew and Christian that the world is created by God and as such is changeable, temporal, and contingent. God, for Aristotle, was separate from, unrelated to, and unknowing of the world. This was opposed not only by the notion of God as creator and sustainer of the world, but more emphatically by the Christian doctrine of God and person that came out of the trinitarian controversies. A third opposition, while not specifically Christian, is about the conception of "being"; on the one hand Aristotle views being as more of an abstract essence, whereas, in the interpretation of some, Thomas Aquinas understands being as the act of existing. In each of the above cases there is some form of opposition, whether by way of negation, revision, or change, which results in some influencing and molding of the key notions of "world," "God," "person," and "being."

A common characteristic that allows us to speak of a Hebrew-Christian tradition is the special place that is given to "person." In the first place there is the relation of God to humans that is personal, not only because God is creator, but especially because he is sustainer of the world. It is this continuing daily relation, not only an originative relation, that explains God as knowing and willing about the world. The notion of person is seen as even more central to the conception of God in the Christian doctrine of the Trinity. This doctrine explains that Jesus is divine insofar as he is one in nature with God. The distinction is a distinction of person. God, who is one in divine nature, is several in person. Three divine persons in one divine nature is the doctrine of the Trinity. The Gospel of John tells us that in the Trinity God is the very reason or rationality of the world. "In the beginning was the Word [i.e., the Logos—second person of the one God]: the Word was with God and the Word was God. . . .Through him all things came to be, not one thing had its being but through him. All that came to be had life in him. . . ." The Incarnation is the embodiment of the Word, the second person of the one God, in human nature. Jesus, the Christ, is the Word or second divine person with both a divine nature and a human nature. Jesus is the rationality of God. God in the person of Jesus has given reality and existence to humans and the world they live in. The theological exposition of the Trinity (three persons in one divine nature) and the Incarnation (hypostatic union—one divine person and both divine nature and human nature) could be developed only in relation to the concept of person. The theology became articulated amid much controversy and many divergent theories. Augustine of Hippo, though not the principal figure of this development, profited from the controversy; his world view about God, humans, and their relations reveals the development in thought that results from the controversy.

## AUGUSTINE OF HIPPO

Augustine, to illustrate the previous point, argues that humans are most specially subjects, not just objects, and if they are to be known and understood then it is as such that they are to be known. Where Plato and Aristotle would ask the question: What is a human being? Augustine asks in the first place: Who am I? This is not only a shift of emphasis or starting point, but also a change of focus. The first question for the Greeks assumes that there is a fixed order of which humans are a part, and they are to be known in this arrangement. The question Augustine is asking does not regard humans as merely part of a wider scheme of all things. It rather sees human centeredness as the starting point and the focal point to which all else is secondarily related. It holds the preeminence of human questioning as a uniquely different value that sets the human person off from the world. The person is unique because it is a conscious being. As conscious it is most of all a subject, a self, rather than an object among other things of a like dimension. In its consciousness the person is knowing and willing. But these activities, though a mark of uniqueness, also show that a human can decide and fail, or know and yet refuse to use this knowledge. Such traits reveal the contingent character of humans. The traits can be used to set humans off from the objective world, but Augustine rather uses the contingent character to show what a human person is and how different humans are from the divine. It is this latter that Augustine sees as the prime relation to be set as the center of all knowledge and life. In short, rather than start with objects and their relations, and humans as part of this, Augustine sees himself as a person and as such related to God as a person, and through this relation he sees himself and other humans, and only then himself and things of the world. The suggestion being made is that this is a different base for a philosophical system, and further, that it is the outcome from the trinitarian and Christological controversies of the early Christian era.

This unique turn in the history of thought is reflected in Augustine's style of writing, in the type of argument he uses, and in the sorts of questions he considers. His style of writing is revealed, for example, when he asks: Who am I? rather than: What is a human being? Even more intimate and revealing is the continuing use of the personal pronoun "I"—the first person rather than the third person, least of all the completely impersonal "it." Finally, in his writings Augustine constantly includes personal prayer to a personal God. This is a frequent reminder that he himself and God are central; everything else is to be regarded as secondary.

An illustration of the sort of argument Augustine uses can be found in his refutation of skepticism, the argument that Descartes paralleled about twelve centuries later. Augustine's technique of refutation is not simply to deliver an absolute denial, but rather to construct a minimal refutation. This is done by taking the most sensitive point of the skeptical position and directing the refutation at this point. Augustine finds the most sensitive point of the skeptical position is about one's own existence; it is not about existence in general, the objective and impersonal, although all of this later is part of the skeptical doubt or denial. Secondly, Augustine hypothetically grants the first move of the skeptic, namely, I can be mistaken. The crucial point is to show that even if what they, the skeptics, wish to assert is true, their own conclusion does not follow. Rather, the conclusion that follows contradicts what they, the skeptics, wish to establish.

In two ways this argument illustrates Augustine's attachment to the preeminence of the personal. First, it concentrates on the conscious self or subject as the area of concern for the argument. The results of the argument, if successful, can then be extended to the objective world. It is not the other way around. Secondly, this argument is one from self-contradiction, namely, that the position of the skeptics falls apart from within as inconsistent. This is an indication of the strongest form of reflexive thinking, that is, making a position apply to itself. As a mode of argumentation it demands a twofold movement of thought, namely, being aware of what the position is about, and also making the position itself part of what the position is about. For example, if one says that everything is false, then I can ask in addition if this declarative statement itself is also false; and if it is, then I need pay no attention to it; if it is not, then it is opposed to the claim being made.

Augustine's attachment to the personal and the human subject is illustrated by the sorts of philosophical questions that he considers. He gives lengthy treatment to such topics as human memory and time. The analysis of "time" is a good illustration. Augustine uses a reflexive mode of analysis and treats common concepts and expressions for self-consistency or self-contradiction. For example, he takes the common assumption that time is made up of three parts: past, present, and future. But it cannot be that the past exists, because it is past only when it exists no longer. Nor can it be that the future exists, because it is future only when it does not yet exist. Consequently, what looked like a handy way of dividing up an answer to the question: What is time? shows that instead of three parts there is only one, namely, the present. Moreover, if one subdivides the present it can fragment into instantaneous nonexistent nothings that are past, that is, nonexistent, before they are realized. As a general result Augustine tentatively suggests an analysis of time that does not fragment the present and that treats the past as a present view of the past and the future as a present expectation of things to come.

This topic, the analysis of time, is important first of all because God, who is eternal and as such outside the temporal order, yet personal and related to humans, must be able to enter into and affect the temporal order. And so God as person is both outside of time and yet in knowledge and action in time. In addition, humans, who as persons are subject to change, show their temporal character in their contingency and mortality. Yet God's promise, as a person, through the Scriptures, is immortality, which is to be understood as not simply life after death but unending existence after death. The human person who begins in time by creation stretches out through time without ending. Finally, the world which is created has a beginning from nothing; it is the most abrupt transition possible—from nothing to something. The sense of time is at the center of the conception of the world as created. The sense of the world and time for the Christian is different from Greek conceptions of the world. For the Greek, time is cyclical, always different, but never far removed from the past or the future. For the Christian, the sense of time is linear, in that it has a beginning which is unique and nonrepeatable; it also has a direction. It is the moment, the now, the present, that has meaning, value, and importance. In the same way the world which had a beginning and is temporal can be otherwise and can end. This contingent character of the world is so manifest to Augustine that it is part of his own life-experience. There is no ultimate value to be attached to the world or to the material. It is above all in mind or soul that humans are to be prized and to be likened to God.

One final reminder. It is possible so to stress or center on the self or the subject as the central focus of Augustine's views that one comes to regard them as purely personal, subjective, or arbitrary. This would be inaccurate. For Augustine the self, subject, or human person, is the central focus; it is never objective, nor is it subjective in the sense of being private or arbitrary. Augustine's reflections are carried on in the spirit of saying, "This is me, isn't it the same for you?" It might be better to call this *inter*-subjective, because it is carried on between or among human subjects. It is not arbitrary, because Augustine is firmly convinced that the structure of thought is the structure of the world.

## ANSELM OF CANTERBURY

Anselm of Canterbury is introduced here because of a famous argument which he proposed for the existence of God. The argument is highly controversial; many persons famous in the history of philosophy have taken sides regarding it or its related forms. For example, such an unlikely grouping of philosophers as Thomas Aquinas, Immanuel Kant, and Bertrand Russell, to name a few, are joined in offering specific refutations of the argument, whereas philosophers such as Descartes, Spinoza, and Hegel, to mention only a few, have made important use of related versions of the argument. In our own day the argument continues to draw attention from several who have made contemporary reformulations of it in either formal logical symbolization or developments of linguistic theory.

The argument as it is found in Anselm has at least the tenuous connection with Augustine in that it presupposes a necessary relation between thought and reality. The argument assumes that if it can be shown that certain connections are necessarily made in thought, then they must also exist in reality. However, in other respects the argument is not so much a continuation of Augustine as it is a development beyond his thought. Anselm is concerned with a personal God, with one who is the object of his belief and to whom he delivers personal prayer, but his overarching concern is to formulate a logical argument that will show why impersonal reason convinces all to hold to the existence of God.

The technique of the argument is to start with the meanings of the terms involved and proceed from an analysis of them to the existence of God. It is called "ontological" because it moves from "being" ["on," "ontos"] to existence. If the argument holds, then it tells us some very important things about the nature of existence. It is an argument because there is an identifiable starting point, and from this there are steps to a conclusion. The premises differ from the conclusion but are connected to the conclusion, so that if the premises are true the conclusion follows and is also true.

It is not very difficult to identify the specifics of the argument in the text of Anselm's *Proslogium*. Literally, Anselm's starting point is "belief" in a being "than which nothing greater can be conceived." A translation of this rather difficult phrase and one that is considerably easier to work with is "a most perfect being." The first step beyond Anselm's starting point is the existence in the understanding of this "most perfect being." The next step is to point out that this is equivalent to mental existence of this most perfect being. The third step is the discovery that real existence is more than mental existence. The conclusion from steps one and three is that the "most perfect," which is "most," is both mentally and really existing.

There are many criticisms and/or refutations that can be offered. Four sensitive areas of the argument will be considered. In the first place, Anselm's starting point of *belief* in such a being is not universally shared and at least seems to be begging the very point that the argument is constructed to establish. This difficulty, though real, is a difficulty with the start Anselm uses. But his start can be bypassed as only historically, not essentially, linked to the argument. One can just as easily start with step one: the *understanding* of [not the belief in] a "most perfect being." This suggestion, if accepted, avoids the problems of belief but does have its own problems. Two sorts of people accept this first step of Anselm's argument—those who affirm and those who deny. Those who deny, to be able to deliver an effective denial, must understand what they are denying. This somewhat obvious point is the clever part of Anselm's technique. However, there is still the very serious difficulty, seemingly not considered by Anselm, of the objection of those who do not understand and claim no more than that they do not know "a most perfect being." In a word, Anselm considers the possibilities of believers and atheists but overlooks agnostics. For this last sort of person there is no way to begin the argument, and if no beginning, then no conclusion can be drawn.

The move in the argument from the first step (understanding) to the second step (mental existence) seems inoffensive and will have no further comment. A third sensitive area of the argument is the third step. This area has drawn, perhaps, the most comment. Some wish to deny that existence is a perfection; consequently, the premise that real existence is more than mental existence is false. Or, others—and this is essentially the criticism of Kant—point out that "being is not a predicate" and consequently "existence" adds nothing to the concept of something. Without getting into the technicalities of the counterarguments that have developed over the centuries, we may offer the brief comment that some say that the Kantian approach has become a slogan and needs content backing; in the same way, the point the argument is trying to make with this premise also remains undeveloped.

A final sensitive area of the argument is the conclusion. The attack of Thomas Aquinas is directed here. Aquinas points out that the conclusion proves no more than that if you can think of a most perfect being then such a being must be *thought of* as both really existing and mentally existing. The proof, so the objection goes, does not conclude to extra-mental actual existence, but only to the need to think about such a being as if it were really existing.

The controversy about the argument has not lessened, but it has been reformulated by those who, in a recent popular move, point out that most refutations have been directed against only the first part of Anselm's text. There is, in addition, a second ontological argument that is immune to the standard criticisms. Both Hartshorne and Malcolm, two contemporary philosophers, have given more technical reformulations of this second argument of Anselm. They point out the second argument does not deal with "perfection" but with "necessary existence." The strategy of the argument is to set up contradictories between the necessity, on the one hand, or the impossibility, on the other, of a necessary being. Further, Anselm argues that such a being cannot be impossible. He concludes that this being necessarily exists.

Anselm does consider and eliminate any third possibility to the two contradictories that he sets up. This takes care of one kind of objection that can be made. Secondly, Findlay, a recent writer, and others have argued, somewhat following Hume, that necessary existence is impossible. Therefore, the choice among the contradictory alternatives is wrongly made by Anselm. As a matter of fact, the argument proves that a necessary being is impossible and, consequently, this is an argument for atheism rather than for the existence of God. At the core of this objection is the central question of being and existence and also of metaphysics insofar as it is concerned with them. The question is: What is the nature of existence? One view, for example that of Hume, maintains that all existence is contingent and so all talk about necessary existence is nonsense. A recent phrasing of this objection is that experience limits or bounds our conceptual or linguistic capabilities; our experience is only of the contingent; consequently, any claims to speak of more than the contingent are pseudo-claims. An opposed view is to grant that there is the experience of contingent existence and the truth that at least some existence is contingent. But to speak of contingent existence is to presuppose that at least some existence is necessary. Thomas Aquinas, in his "third way," makes use of this sort of argument.

## THOMAS AQUINAS

Thomas Aquinas is a main representative of the period of the Middle Ages. He more than any other made the period what it was both in its philosophy and in its theology. He was a member of a religious order. An important difference between him and his contemporaries is that he has a close affinity to Aristotle, rather than to Plato and the various schools of Platonism. Part of the spirit of the times was to write commentaries on the writings of recognized masters. This custom indicated respect for one's predecessors and also provided the writer an occasion to exercise both his interpretive and his critical skills. These commentaries are not simply repetitions of standard opinions; in some cases, as in that of Aquinas, they are the vehicle of some original thinking. Aquinas is recorded as writing that "authority is the weakest of arguments," and again that "authority has a wax nose," meaning thereby that it can be twisted and turned to one's own liking and needs.

An example of a commentary is the writing Aquinas did about Aristotle's *Metaphysics*. To introduce the commentary, Aquinas wrote a prologue. Here he shapes the direction of his interpretation of Aristotle in a discussion of various names given to metaphysics. Aquinas shows in the prologue that he holds in common with Aristotle that all knowledge has a hierarchical structure with singleness, metaphysics, at the apex by which all else is ruled and governed. Both Aquinas and Aristotle reveal an intellectualist bias in holding that this study is the most intellectual insofar as it is certain, and about the causes. Aquinas adds that it is about the first cause and so it gets the name of "first philosophy." Both Aristotle and Aquinas show a generalist's bias by preferring the general over the specific. Since "being" is the most general of all notions, Aquinas adds that this study is called "metaphysics." This name was unknown to Aristotle, but for Aquinas it is both a place location and a proper name. Finally, both Aristotle and Aquinas show an immaterialist's bias in preferring the immaterial to the material. What is separate from matter is more closely allied to this subject matter, and consequently it gets the name of "divine science" or "theology." Both of these names are also found in Aristotle's writings, but the emphasis is on the subject matter as most like to what the divine being would do, whereas for Aquinas it also has the connotation that what is studied leads up to the divine being.

Whereas the generalities about metaphysics are treated in the prologue, it is the individual books of the commentary that explore the specifics. For example, Book Delta of the *Metaphysics* is one of the main places where Aristotle speaks of the various senses of "being." Aquinas's commentary can be carefully compared with Aristotle's text and shows in general basic agreement between the two with some small though important variations. Aristotle's analysis of the four senses of "being" results in a preference for the second sense of "being." It is the "being" of the categories and primarily substance which Aristotle holds as its main sense. Aquinas also calls this sense of "being," "complete being." Furthermore, both Aristotle and Aquinas agree that "being" is of various kinds because of the variety of ways of predication, that is, because of the various ways something is said of a subject. For example, a predicate can tell us "what" a thing is, a "what kind of," "how much," etc. Only the first of these sorts of predicates, "what it is," is first substance, particular substance, or the existing individual. All of these are considered by Aristotle to be basically equivalent, and in Book Gamma of the *Metaphysics* he holds that "man" and "existing man" signify the same. This, because it is ambiguous, leaves open the interpretation that for Aristotle there is no basic difference between an essence and an existing essence, or, to intensify the ambiguity, between a possible essence and an existing essence. Some have held that if this interpretation is correct then metaphysics is to be considered as the study of the possibles, with existence subsumed underneath possible being as a part of a wider subject. But conversely, Aristotle can be interpreted as holding that the existing individual is first substance and this is the prime sense of "being." This is the same as holding that "man" and "existing man" are the same because the first is appropriated to and reduced to the second. However, the first interpretation is that "existing man" is reducible to "man"; consequently, "first substance," which is the prime meaning of "being," is "*what* a thing is" or the essence.

Aquinas commits himself to *existing* "being" as the complete sense of "being." In working from predication to substance Aquinas says, "In all predication something is signified to be." From texts such as this some point out that Aquinas reads *being* as a participle, signifying the act of existing, the "to be" of a thing as the meaning of "being." This sense is in place of "being" as a noun, a thing, an essence. In the mentioned interpretation Aquinas holds esse not *ens* as the meaning of "being." Actuality not possibility is the subject matter of metaphysics.

"Esse" signifies dynamically; it is not a noun which would reify being and conceive it as an essence. It is a verb, and it signifies not an essence but the act which is the "to be" of substance. "Esse," for Aquinas, in this interpretation, is what is most central in the existing thing.

"Being" considered in this way has important implications for the concepts of "God" and "world," which are two of the other three key concepts of this chapter. God, who is a being, is unlimited existence for Aquinas. Otherwise put, the position is that God's essence is his existence. The world is created, and each created thing is limited; the principle of limitation is essence, namely, the creature is limited to be this sort of thing and not something else. What a thing is (essence) makes (limits) each created thing to be (existence) this thing. But God, pure existence, is unlimited because there is in him no essence, no "what," to limit existence pure and simple. It is this view of "being" which makes understandable the radical distinction between God as creator and the world as created. Though "being," "God," and "world" all signify and function in the metaphysics of Aristotle, they signify and function in a very different way in the metaphysics of Aquinas.

We have already looked at the notion of "person" and the changes that occurred in relation to the exposition of the doctrine of the Trinity and the Incarnation in Christianity. These changes are reflected in the writings of Augustine in his ideas about both God and the world. They are also reflected in his style of writing, with its heavy emphasis on the first person approach. As a point of difference, the first person style of writing is not used by Aquinas. In writings other than his commentaries he uses the impersonal style of logical argumentation, which reflects the popular dialectical style of medieval scholastic disputation. Successively following from a statement of the question are the objections, the position of the author, and finally, answers to the objections. This format allows presentation of full scope of the issue and helps avoid onesidedness. Because such a format is impersonal, it might be considered a regression in relation to the human person; but, on the other hand, it could also be shown to be a fully conscious and reflective style that is an interpersonal mode of expression. Provided that the presence of proofs and full scale argumentation is recognized as the vital life blood of philosophy, then the personal style seems not to be the main mode of philosophical writing.

Aquinas does display full allegiance to argumentation, and his two *Summa*'s are packed with arguments pro and con. The doctrine of God as a cornerstone of his system is integrated into his total world view and has specific arguments in support of this view. The integration is so close that it is demanded by parts of the system for completeness. Some say that the arguments proposed in the sections about God are not to be regarded as full fledged proofs standing independently but rather are sketches to show the rational basis of belief in God. First we will consider the existence of God, and then the integration of the doctrine of God into the system.

Only two objections to the existence of God are mentioned by Aquinas, but they are regarded, even in our time, as two of the most powerful ones. Other objections can be constructed; at least these are representative and primary candidates on any list. The first objection is that evil in the world is incompatible with "goodness" which is part of the meaning of "God." Perhaps a third premise is needed to the effect that omnipotence or all-powerfulness is also proper to God. The sense of the objection remains the same. God means goodness; evil is real; this latter cancels out God. The technique Aquinas uses in answering the objection is not to deny the existence of evil. He rather grants the reality of physical evils but denies that evil is the final result. He holds that evil brings about goodness, or, ultimately goodness triumphs. It is clear that this exchange is not a complete treatment of the problem of evil. It should be understood that Aquinas's total treatment would include the doctrine of immortality or that life is not exhausted by what happens between birth and death, and, at least for a believing Christian, one must take into account the many implications of the crucifixion and resurrection of Jesus. If these additional doctrines are included, then it is plausible to accept this article of the *Summa* as a sketch which fits into and hence is only part of a wider, total, systematic view of the world.

The second objection is that God is superfluous and not needed to account for what happens in the world. The objection holds that two elements alone, nature and humans, are sufficient to have a complete view of the world and its events. Once again Aquinas grants the starting point that nature and humans do explain what happens, but he adds that to have a complete understanding and a total picture some account must also be given of the two crucial elements, namely, nature and humans. He goes on to point out that since neither nature nor humans are self-justifying, then the first cause of these must be included for the total picture.

For his positive presentation on the existence of God, Aquinas chooses to call each of the five sections "ways," not proofs or demonstrations. Some hold that this signifies that they are not to be regarded as having logically final completeness. Whatever the answer may be, here there is only a brief indication of the structure of each of the "ways" and its problem areas.

The structure of the first way can be analyzed as follows: There is a starting point which is empirical, and the evidence for this is in sense experience. The second move is to go out of or beyond sense experience. The third premise is to stop this movement outside or to keep it from continuing without limit. The conclusion follows from these three premises to the effect that there is a "first" or ultimate source of whatever you have started with. In the case of the first way, Aquinas starts from the sensory fact of change. He proceeds to point out that change comes from outside of or beyond what does change. The process of locating the source of change outside of the changing cannot go on without end. The conclusion is that there is a first source of change.

The starting point of the first way is not one of the main problem areas; it is relatively noncontroversial. Perhaps that is why Aquinas calls this the most obvious of the five ways. Objection can be made to the second premise with examples of self-moving, self-perfecting devices. Indeed, one characterization of life in general is that it consists in being capable of immanent, self-perfective activity. Aquinas tries to hedge against this objection by pointing out that what is changing either has or does not have what is happening. If the first, then it is not changing and not the case in question. If the second, then what happens comes from other than what is changing, and this is the point he wishes us to grant. The third premise is needed to eliminate an infinite series. Aquinas eliminates an infinite series by means of subordination and dependence of the result on its cause. To extend the line of causes indefinitely as an infinite series requires would not only rule out a first cause but also eliminate all the members of the subsequent series which are subordinate to and dependent on the first cause. But the first premise has already acknowledged the existence of the subordinate members, and their existence cannot now be ruled out. If they exist, then the first cause must exist. The final problem area is the conclusion. It could be that one could admit the conclusion but point out that this first cause of change is impersonal and unrelated to any substantial conception of God. Aquinas does not consider such an objection, but he could respond by granting the objection and pointing out that what is established is minimal, though not incompatible with more substantial conceptions of God.

The details of the analysis of the first of the five ways of Aquinas are worth the effort spent in mastering them. The second way follows exactly the same model as the first way. There is an empirical starting point, two additional premises which are almost exactly the same as the corresponding ones in the first way, and a conclusion. The third way follows the standard model set up in the first two ways. But there is an important difference. Aquinas does not only establish that something must be or that there is a necessary being; he must also establish that there is a being whose necessity is from itself. The reason for this extra step in the third way is that Aquinas, as odd as it may seem to us, held that there were several sorts of necessary beings; among these are souls, prime matter, and angels.

The fourth way is much different from the others. It has been called Platonic and hence based in a world view that Aquinas does not adopt. For such a reason it is frequently disregarded. Its basic point is that wherever there are degrees of more or less, then there must be most or superlative. The top, or most perfect, controls all that share in the common character. The difficulties with this sort of argument are in identifying perfections and defects without reading one's own personal values into the proof.

The fifth way makes use of final cause or goal, which is the other extrinsic Aristotelian cause. The first three ways make use of efficient cause, and they look to origins, whereas the fifth way, using final cause, looks to results. It is not the argument from design; in other words, it does not argue that all the pieces fit together in some harmonious scheme such as the clockwork of the heavens. It has an empirical starting point, namely, that we discover that things observe, for example, developmental laws so that various phases of growth unfold in orderly succession. Each tends to a goal which is not an accidental happening. Direction comes from a being with awareness and understanding. Therefore, there is a director.

Various forms of this proof have been around for a long time. Kant calls it "the oldest, clearest" and "most in conformity with the common reason humanity." It "deserves to be mentioned with respect." Yet there are many sensitive problem areas with it. For example, some might be willing to grant the conclusion drawn but point out that it is not strong enough to prove the existence of a God but only of a very great intelligence. Or, it may be pointed out that the proof does not establish a single intelligence because a committee could just as easily be fitted into the conclusion. Again, the conclusion does not allow us to hold that the director is still on duty because he could have completed his work and gone elsewhere or ceased to exist. One of the strongest criticisms comes from the theory of evolution and makes the point that evolution and its mechanisms, as far as they are known to us, e.g., natural selection by means of survival of the fittest, or such like, explain the goal-seeking of organisms. If so, the facts alleged in the proof may not need the conclusion that there is a conscious being with knowledge and power. A final strong internal criticism would come from those who wish completely to eliminate teleology as a mode of understanding or explaining nature. This view will be discussed at greater length when the impact of natural science on philosophy is considered.

Aquinas's total view of the world is that it is ordered and structured. God is supreme in this order and structure. All else is regarded as coming from and ordered to God. God enters into the world not as a part of it but as separate from it. How does he enter? First of all as creator, source, and efficient cause. God as cause is separate from the effect which is outside himself. But this also provides the link which is that of the imprint of the cause on its effect. God, besides being efficient cause, is also final cause in regard to the world. God stays with the world as its goal, its tendency, its direction. This latter sort of causality is more difficult to establish. For Aquinas it is at least implicit, if not explicit, and at least secondary, if not primary. The argument he gives is that a rational creature who is conscious and knowing alone can do the tracing of connections. The tracing is done by analysis of what is secondary and implicit as dependent on the primary and explicit. The connections are either of subordination, namely, the secondary is known as secondary only when the primary is known and identified; or there can be likeness, namely, that which exists in one member is seen as resembling and connected to another. For example, to desire life is to desire implicitly God as the fullness of life and existence, both as its source and its goal. All life is secondary and derivative of divine life to which it bears at least faint similarities.

The complete doctrine of Aquinas needs the integration of God into his world view. Such an integration can be done only by changes and developments in the conceptions of "God," "world," "person," and "being." All of these key concepts have, in some cases slight, in others major, differences from the way they are used by his Greek predecessors. Although Aquinas sees three names of metaphysics, he has a preference for the name of "divine science" or "theology." This means that for him metaphysics has its highest development insofar as it studies separated substances and has a separation from matter. This is existence pure and simple, unrestricted, not limited to a "what" or by an essence. This is be-ing or the "to be." The highest activity of humans is in the exercise of knowing by intellect because then the resemblance is strongest with the divine and the separation from matter is clearest. Humans, however, remain creatures; that is, their existence is limited as particular kinds of being with emotions and passions which among other things are clear instances of our embodied nature. Humans share with the world in their createdness, finiteness, and contingency. They are also elevated above the world by the study of metaphysics, which both leads them toward God as source and destination, and helps them to be godlike.

# III
# THE MODERNS

The objective of this chapter is to enumerate some of the important philosophical developments that took place during the periods known as the Renaissance and the Enlightenment. In brief, the main influences bringing about the changes were on the one hand the developing natural sciences and on the other new views of the task of philosophy.

The term "Renaissance" as used here is to be understood as neither that entire time period nor everything that comes under that title. For example, if it were to include the cultural Renaissance in its literary and artistic aspects, then the time period would be too vast. The writings of Petrarch and the paintings of Giotto in Italy were occurring about the same time as the writings of Thomas Aquinas. These early cultural stirrings of the Renaissance are related in time to the Middle Ages. The literary and artistic aspects of the Renaissance also share for the most part the basic presuppositions of classical philosophy, such as belief in an objective world separable from humans. For these reasons "Renaissance" is used here not in its most general and unrestricted sense, but rather refers to the scientific Renaissance as that term is used to refer to the developing natural sciences. The natural sciences were a main influence on much of what occurred in philosophy from the fifteenth until the nineteenth century.

At the start, Renaissance science progressed in reference to astronomy, both in the theories, such as that of Copernicus about the relationship of the earth and the other heavenly bodies and in the development of various instruments, such as the telescope, for the observation and collection of data. The concepts of "world" that are involved are not simply in transition from flat-earth to sphere-world conceptions, nor from geocentric to sun as one of many star-centered systems. The changes were more basic and might be better expressed as the replacement of the view of the world as closed and bounded with the conception of the open universe. Consider the view of those who maintain that the Copernican theory that the world was not the center of the heavenly bodies dealt a devastating blow to the ego of humans. This view holds that humans could no longer feel that everything was placed in relation to earth and that they were not the most magnificent of all creatures. But is it true to say that the Copernican theory was an affront to human dignity? Perhaps, if humans thought of their greatness as one of physical position. But human significance is not measured by size of body, length of history, physical ability, or such like. The Copernican revolution would have us adopt a sun-centered instead of a geocentric view because such a theory fits the facts better than any other, especially the Ptolemaic which it replaced. Even deeper, the lesson of the Copernican theory was that humans by their understanding could know how things stood—knowledge is power and a way to dominate the world. No longer was one bound to earth and closed in. While infinity of the universe was not only staggering but a conceptual impossibility to humans, there was still a breaking of the bonds of a closed world and its replacement by an open universe.

In addition to the new astronomy and its influence on the view of the world, there was an even more important development in the sciences. Mathematical techniques, both arithmetic and geometry, were applied to the fields of astronomy and physics. This application was the mainspring of the development of the sciences. Whereas passive observation or active experimentation might be the initial stimulus or even the final test, it was the use of mathematics that enabled the study, for example of astronomy, to develop as an organized body of knowledge. One illustration was the attempt to discover the mechanism governing the observed speed-up and slow-down of a heavenly body in its elliptical orbit. The explanation was discovered and considered complete and understandable when the mathematical formula expressing a numerical relation could be given. This is Kepler's Second Law, and it describes mathematically the speed of a planet in an elliptical orbit around the sun. This speed is equal to the area covered by the sweep of an imaginary line drawn between the sun and the planet. In this example there is both the unity of mathematical simplicity and observational accuracy. Such characteristics as these became part of the new model of understanding and explaining the world. The example is not an isolated one. Gravitation was explained by a numbering of distance and weight, and by the application of a formula. The world was no longer understood in terms of quality, but rather by quantity and quantifiable relations that can be abstractly plotted. Obervation and experimentation feed the initial data and conduct the governing check, but the central part of the explanation is mathematical. This new mode of explanation as a way of understanding the world replaced the older conception of classical philosophy which sought for essences and formal causes. The new way of science rejected formal causes and essences as being a search for hidden characteristics. The objectivity of the natural sciences consists in expressing the results in arithmetical measure, mathematical relations, or a description of what a thing does, that is, its functions. The new mode of understanding and explanation which emphasizes the use of a mathematical model and quantity and quantification techniques is more than ever true today, e.g., the application of computers to decision theory.

Some of the results of these new developments in the natural sciences had influence in the field of philosophy. The Aristotelian doctrine of essences, of formal cause, was rejected. Likewise, there was a rejection of final cause, teleology; a substitution of a dynamic mode of exposition and the importance of operative qualities, i.e., what a thing does, its functions; a rejection of the doctrine of natural place in favor of the concept of inertia, i.e., continued motion or continued rest; and the elimination of the distinction of the celestial from the terrestrial.

Besides rejecting formal cause and essences, Renaissance science also rejected final cause, which had been so important to Aristotle. The rejected mode of understanding viewed the world in terms of purpose or goal. Its model was that of conscious humans; its terms were those of motivation consciously conceived beforehand, which was extended to life and living things. For the medievals it was extended to nonliving things by means of the finger of God. An exaggerated example would be the explanation that the North Star was so placed in the heavens to guide sailors at night. This is an exaggeration, but it does illustrate an earth-centered viewpoint. It is teleology run wild; it is anthropomorphism in the sense of conceiving the inanimate world as if it had human form and human modes of values and interests. Renaissance science consciously rejected teleology as applied to the nonliving; some later science rejected its application to life in general; most recently there is the behavioristic rejection of the assessment of motives as a mode of explanation. All these share a common rejection of the inner, private, and unobservable; they substitute the outer, public, measurable, and quantifiable.

Opposed to the view that nature is a grouping of things is the view of Renaissance science that nature is a process, an interrelation and interaction of never-the-same-again entities. Only functional exposition can accommodate this dynamic view of the world. It is outer and public, and it describes what a thing does. It can handle a process; in astronomy, for example, it can handle the movement of planets in a system. It is opposed to a static view in which each reality is a thing which when rigid and stable is understandable.

The older doctrine was that of natural place; heavy things fall because their natural place is down at the center of the earth, whereas heat rises because its natural place is up, and things get progressively purer as they are up. The new science substituted the concept of inertia, in which there was continued movement or continued rest unless outside forces intervened.

A final noteworthy change eliminated the distinction between celestial or heavenly on the one hand and the terrestrial or earthly on the other. There is a common material composition in the universe. It is not that everything is the same bland neutral stuff, but rather that what is found here is also found elsewhere in the universe.

The laws, the material composition, the mode of explanation as common, all these allow literally a uni-verse—a "oneness" rather than four elements here and fifth or quintessence elsewhere in the heavens. All these discoveries were knowledge, power, and the glorification of humans and their abilities. Renaissance science was a heady, optimistic experience that resulted in the exaltation of humans and their abilities.

In addition to the developing natural sciences in the time of the Renaissance, some major changes took place in the conception of the task of philosophy. The phrase, "the task of philosophy," is rather vague. There never was agreement on what such a task might be. In fact, different conceptions were probably a great source of controversy and nonagreement. However, despite controversy and diversity, some generalities can be expressed. During this time period the central focus of philosophy was not the world, as it had been for some of the Greeks, nor its composition, structure, or laws of interaction. The world in its public, experimentable aspects was the realm of the natural sciences. Nor was the central focus of philosophy God, as it was for some of the medievals. It was not the agent or first efficient cause, or God as model, or God as final goal at the consummation of the world. God as transcendent was for religion and theology. Yet both the world as nonscientific and God as nonreligious are considered to be a part of philosophy. But the central focus was neither the world nor God. It was man, the human person. The Renaissance gave birth to a form of humanism. This humanism or man-centeredness was the focus of philosophy, which thus became mainly the study of humans as nonempirical and as nontranscendent.

The philosophical humanism of the scientific Renaissance was not naively optimistic. In the first place it expressed doubts about the knowing powers of humans. In good part the work of the new science consisted in rejecting the unsubstantiated claims that had been carried on through the history of the human race. The power and limits of knowing were taken seriously. The first epistemological task of philosophy was to set the bounds of knowing so that the entire edifice of knowledge was not hollow and unsupported. This task when completed would then give limits to, and the extent of, "being" and "existence."

Of the specific philosophers considered in this chapter each reacted in a radically different way to the developments in the natural sciences, to the changing conceptions of the task of philosophy; and each reacted in his own way to his predecessors and contemporaries in the field of philosophy. A fragmentation occurred in philosophy. Each philosopher almost stands alone. Each could be considered alone except for the very generalized characteristics of being influenced by the developments in the natural sciences and of reacting to other philosophers. The specific influence and the specific reaction in each case was as unlike as are the personalities of the men.

The name "modern" is given to philosophy from about the fifteenth century because, even though there is some continuity with the medievals, there are important differences from the older philosophical tradition. The differences are not all true of any one philosopher, but at least some are true of each. More differences occur in those later in the period, for example, more in Kant than in Descartes. One of the differences was in the form of literary expression. For example, whereas the medievals wrote in Latin, beginning with the Renaissance the vernacular was used with increasing frequency. The medievals frequently used the commentary on standard works as a form of expression, but the moderns almost exclusively wrote original treatises. A second, somewhat external, difference was that philosophy emerged from the confines of the schools. The medievals were for the most part university professors, who taught in the schools where there was a traditional, fixed curriculum. The moderns in the majority of cases were unconnected with academic teaching. The philosophy they wrote was a matter of common interest and concern for the educated classes. But later, with Kant and thereafter, philosophy became technical and abstruse; a developed skill was needed to handle it. The major difference, an intrinsic difference, was that philosophy for the moderns became autonomous. The autonomy was twofold, both as a separate branch of study and as an area of concern free from theological themes. It was not so much that the natural sciences replaced theology as the dominant influence on philosophy; the natural sciences pursued their own path of development that separated from philosophy. But it is true that psychology, at this time, was not considered separate from philosophy. Some, like Hume, proposed a study of man that would be a science to match what was happening in chemistry, physics, etc. Descartes and Spinoza treated extensively of the emotions. Locke and Hume mixed the psychological and epistemological by asking questions like, How do ideas arise?

The natural sciences were linked to philosophy in their influence upon the direction of philosophical interest. The sorts of questions asked and the standards by which an answer was judged satisfactory were shaped by what was happening in the scientific movement. For the scientifically minded the answers were mathematical and quantitative. In the case of the world, the view of science was that it was a mechanical system that operated by laws of efficient causality. True, one could still ask where was the human. But was it possible to make a place for the human, or was this too to be considered simply as physical and mechanical? As the notion of the physical became more rigidly defined and restricted to terms of the quantifiable and to laws of efficient causality, it made room for the position that what was distinctively human was not definable in the same way. One could give the weight, the volume, and even the chemical composition of a human. But what was most personally human, experience and consciousness, was separate from any imaginable quantificational techniques. The conclusion must be that there was something in addition to the material. If it was not material, it was spiritual. If it was in addition to the material, it must be that the human person must be understood as a twoness, the material and the spiritual, the body and the soul or mind.

As philosophy focused on the human person, one of the major problems became the theories explaining the relation of this twoness—the mind-body problem. If substance is still held to be the basic reality, then this substance will not simply be equated with material substance but must be more broadly conceived. Other such moves and changes must be made; all these adaptations are in large part due to what was happening in the natural sciences.

## RENÉ DESCARTES

René Descartes is a good example of one who lived with all the ambiguities of this transitional time. He illustrates the influence of the developing natural sciences. The continuity of Descartes with the medievals is somewhat artificial, in that some of his writings are in Latin. There are also his religious presuppositions, which he wished to retain; he does this by declaring that as he is saying nothing about religion, then nothing in his writings should be interpreted as against his faith. In other words, Descartes had a special compartment for his beliefs as a Christian, which beliefs he set aside and did not integrate into his writings. This is one way of achieving autonomy from religion and theology.

But Descartes was immersed in the scientific movement, and he does not show a philosophy sharply autonomous from the natural sciences. It is only after Descartes's time that we look on him so easily as a philosopher. He might very well have thought of himself as a mathematician and a scientist rather than as a philosopher. He illustrates the influence of the developing natural sciences not only in some of the positive attitudes he has and some adaptations he makes use of, but also in reactions against some scientific doctrines.

In the first place, Descartes reflects a skeptical attitude about human powers of knowing. His experience is that many claims are falsely asserted and many more are never established. His radical skepticism is reflected in both the "dream" doubt, in which all experience is imaginatively treated as if it were a dream, and the "evil genius" doubt, in which we are to consider ourselves as deceived by one who has the power to keep us constantly in error.

Positively, a mathematical model from geometry supplies Descartes with the technique of giving a firm foundation to human knowing. The way to a solid edifice for all human knowing is an incontestable starting point which grounds all else because every other truth is connected to it by strict deductive derivation.

The argument that Augustine used to overcome the skeptics was probably known to Descartes. In brief, the argument is that for any human experience, even those of doubt, deception, and error, there is always one undeniable certainty which is the subject of such an experience. This firm, undeniable first truth gives Descartes the starting point from which he proceeds to deduce the rest of the truths that are needed to give a firm edifice of knowledge. Historically, Descartes proceeded from knowledge of self as subject and the establishment of a criterion of true and false, to proving the existence of God. The criterion and the goodness and reliability of God allowed the eventual reestablishment of what can be known about the total human being and the world. Under all these headings could be subsumed everything that was needed for a complete philosophical system.

The emphasis that Descartes gives to the self, the "cogito," the human person, is an emphasis that separates him from the natural sciences. The human person as considered by Descartes is exempt from modes of investigation open to the natural sciences. Descartes works with a distinction of the material and the mental; the latter member of this distinction is not the same as the spiritual which he considered religious. In one way the human is both the material or physical on the one hand and the experiential or mental on the other. But in another way, since the mental is crucial in that only it can exist without the other, then the human is essentially the mental. Perhaps to Descartes the human being was, all things being equal, a twoness of bodily and mental, but in special circumstances it could be a oneness, namely, the mental. Whatever way we put it, Descartes considered the human person as autonomous from the natural sciences of his day. There is also a second way in which Descartes suggested an autonomy of philosophy from science, and that was in the modes of reflexive thinking that he used. Reflexive thinking, to him, showed that doubt needs a doubter and therefore instead of proceeding to what follows or comes next from a truth Descartes first goes back to what is a necessary precondition for a truth. After this first move to establish the starting point it is true that Descartes uses sequential thought as a procedure.

There are some strange paradoxes that arise from what Descartes has done. A first example is in the move he makes to consider the human person as private and inaccessible. This, he believes, makes a human immune from skepticism on the one hand and the mechanical view of the natural sciences on the other. But it also makes each human person private and accessible only to himself and private from and inaccessible to everyone else. The result is solipsism or the doctrine that oneself alone exists; no one has the right to claim anything more than one's own private experiences. If solipsism is true, then there is no such study as philosophy over and above the natural sciences, nor are there even the natural sciences as public, objective, and equally available to all. A second example of a strange paradox is in the doctrine of substance. Substance, as the basic reality of the world, is not equated with material substance. If it were the case that the basic reality is material substance, then the natural sciences and their techniques would cover everything, and there would be no remainder not covered. For some unknown reason, substance for Descartes is defined as "a thing existing in such a manner that it has need of no other thing in order to exist." So defined, God is the only true substance. But given the cooperation of God there can be two kinds of substance: bodily, whose essence is extension, and mental, whose essence is thought. This distinction also constitutes the distinction of philosophy from the natural sciences: bodily, being the field for investigation by the natural sciences, and mental, being the area for philosophy. But philosophy, which makes the distinction, also cancels the distinction by obliterating both members of the distinction if solipsism is true.

Whether or not these paradoxes are valid for Descartes' thought, it is possible to step back and see that there was emerging in his philosophy the distinction between philosophy and the natural sciences. The empirical is the field of science. The religious is compartmentalized and set aside. Both these moves, then, allow an autonomy to philosophy. The area that philosophy covers remains ambiguous. With Descartes we can see that reflexive thinking and a general systematic overview are still legitimate areas of concern and begin to mark out the autonomy of philosophy.

## GEORGE BERKELEY

The British philosopher George Berkeley gave a different viewpoint on substance. If substance is the fundamental reality, then it appears that there cannot be two sorts of substance. Berkeley believed that a human can speak of himself as *immaterial* or spiritual substance. This posed no difficulty for him. But how, he reasons, can one speak of material substance? The only way one can speak of tables and chairs and the "furniture of the universe" is insofar as it is perceptible. But perception is an experience and not material. If this is so, then to "exist" or "to be" is to be perceived. No claims can be substantiated about the unperceived, for example, the material. If "to be" is "to be perceived," then there is only one kind of substance, and it is immaterial or spiritual.

Berkeley still used substance as the central philosophical concept. But he made a significant move in getting rid of what is non-empirical, namely, what is outside experience and perception. There is no material substance or substratum. The idea of a something that has no perceptible qualities or characteristics, a substratum, an "I know not what," is not a "something" but rather a "nothing." Berkeley showed the influence of the natural sciences in eliminating unknowables, in voiding claims that cannot be substantiated. He believed that he could use an attitude from science to refute pernicious anti-religious forces that fostered materialistic attitudes. Religion triumphed because true science showed that materialism was a false doctrine.

## GOTTFRIED LEIBNIZ

Another unusual view on the nature of substance was proposed by Leibniz. He constructed a systematic view that was total and complete. The doctrine of substance is the key to understanding his philosophical system. Instead of using the word "substance" Leibniz used "monad," and he called his doctrine "monadology." He presented his view in the following way. He begins with a definition of substance and a division of it into simple and compound. He gives an argument that simple substances or unities are the foundational ultimate of everything else. These simples, whatever they may be, he calls "monads." The rest of his system gives the characteristics of these monads and relates to them the essential parts of the system. The unique feature of Leibniz's doctrine on monads is that they are lives, souls, and spirits; since monads are everywhere, then nature is full of life. The view proposed by Leibniz was that life is fundamental to the universe, rather than that life is built up of and secondary to the nonliving. Monads are not only alive but are souls, if they have sensation and memory. If they have reason in addition, then they are spirits. Futher, in Leibniz's proposal the monads were not distinguishable except by internal qualities which are perceptions, that is, their view on the world, and their appetitions, that is, their tendencies. Furthermore, since the monads were neither efficient causes nor effects, they were set in perfect harmony by having their total history within them. Rather than efficient causality it was final causality that was needed to understand their operation.

The doctrine and system of Leibniz is important for several features. In the first place, as a doctrine of substance or the stuff of which everything is made, it is clearly a non-empirical doctrine. There are no observations which are relevant in establishing the view Leibniz proposes, nor are there any which could refute it. Secondly, it is arrived at, at least in part, by logical analysis, namely, granting some features, certain other ones are necessary as logical consequences, or necessary for completeness. Many parts of Leibniz's system are definitional; that is, they are

Free man is one who knows why he does what he does.



proposals. Finally, the influence of mathematics and Leibniz's own contributions to calculus is revealed in the conception of monads as infinitesimals that are self-contained. Nevertheless, Leibniz shows he was still connected to classical philosophy insofar as he integrated the doctrine of final causes into his system.

In addition to the total system, Leibniz's doctrine of space and time shows some important developments in the growing autonomy of the field of philosophy. Leibniz carried on a controversy with Clarke, who was representing Newton's views on space. Newton's opinion was that space was a container in which things are placed and to which they have their relationship. Space in this opinion was something in its own right, and so it is called the doctrine of absolute space. Leibniz opposed this view. He argued that space is not a thing in itself but rather the relations existing among things. In other words, it is not the case that first there is space and then things are positioned in relation to it; rather, in order for there to be space there must first be things; and it is the relation, position, distance, and order among these things that we call space. Leibniz argued that one point does not differ from any other except that there be things to which any point has a different relation from any other point. Once there are several objects, then every point outside them has a unique set of coordinates in relation to the given objects. But if there are no objects, then there are no coordinates. And if no coordinates, then no uniqueness or differentiation of one point from another. Space does not exist unless there are discernible differences.

The doctrine of space that Leibniz holds is reasonable and understandable. Space is not a thing but a relation. The same is true for time. Space is a relation of coexistence; time is a relation of succession, of before and after. A perceiving, conscious subject is needed to reflect on the relations that are given among things. This is a good instance of the application of reflexive thinking in philosophy. A mind is needed to perceive the things and to reflect on, not the things, but the relations among them, and to identify and interpret these relations. Further, this approach shows that we do not multiply entities in the world but become aware that at least some of our important concepts do not have actual objects to which the concepts refer. The extension and further development of this line of thinking was more clearly carried on in the philosophy of Kant.

## IMMANUEL KANT

Leibniz argued for a relational doctrine of space and time in place of the doctrine of absolute space and time. Kant's extension of these moves was the transcendental doctrine of space and time. Leibniz held that real objects which were things in themselves were needed for there to be relations. Transcendental philosophy eliminated things in themselves or noumenal realities. A first start to understand transcendental philosophy can be made with the doctrine of transcendental space. There was a specific problem which brought Kant to the conception of transcendental philosophy. He puzzled over Leibniz's doctrine of space. After several revisions of opinion on the subject, he came to see that relational space was not enough to solve this special problem. A coordinate system used in relational space can spell out most relations among things but it cannot distinguish, for example, a right and a left hand, or a screw with a right-handed thread and one with a left-handed thread, provided one of these was the total universe. Every part is identically positioned in relation to every other part; yet they are different. This is called the problem of the incongruous counterparts. How can this be explained? The relational theory of space such as that of Leibniz cannot handle the difference.

The answer to this problem could be made only after Kant made the transcendental turn which he called his Copernican revolution. It was an interesting choice of a slogan in view of the fact that much of the philosophy of this period developed out of a stimulating contact with scientific development. Literally, "revolution" signifies a full turn of a circle. But a full turn would being one back to the same point. Here, "revolution," as is more frequently meant, is only a half circle which puts everything in reverse relationship. The half circle in Kant's Copernican revolution was the change between thought and mind on the one hand and things and the world on the other. Previous to the revolution Kant held the realist view that the world existed independently and the mind conformed to what was given. But Kant's revolutionary view was that the world is a world because the mind is the way it is. If one is to analyze structures, then it is the structure of the mind that one must discover in order then to discover that there is a world. These mental structures or forms are prior to and independent of anything else. They are objective in that they are exactly the same for any and each human knowing creature.

How does the revolution relate to the problem of the incongruous counterparts? It is not the things that are different by themselves. Rather the mind is so structured that they are different. For example, when one speaks of the spatial dimension of height, the above and below are distinguished according to the position of our own body. Likewise, the front and rear are distinguished by relation to ourselves. The right and left are spoken of by reference to the object's position relative to us. Granting there are other ways of referring to spatial dimensions, it remains clear that when we use right and left, for example, we are using a framework which is wider than the object and one that includes ourselves. At one time Kant thought that this wider framework was absolute space, as Newton held. Later on he came to see that the argument from incongruous counterparts did not support Newton's view and, more importantly, refuted Leibniz's relational theory of space. The right as distinguished from the left of a hand or of a glove does not depend on the positioning of its parts. The relational theory held that the positioning of parts was the sole requirement. Such cases and the right and left of a hand or a glove or a vortex, etc., are called "incongruous counterparts." In the case of hands they are "counterparts" insofar as the parts are arranged the same in reference to each other; but they are "incongruent" insofar as one can never occupy the space of the other. They are judged to be right or left as the case may be in reference to a wider framework outside themselves. Kant holds that the perceiving subject is necessary for this wider framework. He further holds that the form of space is contributed

by the perceiving subject. But space is a characteristic of all objects and events. It follows that a necessary condition of the perception of an object is, in this case, the form of space which is a contribution of the human knower. Space is, then, an appearance, a form of human sensibility, imposed by the mind on a nonspatial reality. Space is not an objective entity at all.

The same is true for time. Time and space constitute the two forms of human sensibility. Their only distinction is that time is the form of inner sense, whereas space is the form of outer sense.

This is the transcendental turn. It is Kant's Copernican revolution, the move to a fully reflexive philosophy. The mind in this move becomes fully aware of itself and its contributions to the activity of knowing. Technically, Kant calls knowledge transcendental when it is about the a priori conditions of the possibility of knowing. In more common language, Kant is seeking for the prior conditions, the presuppositions, or the assumptions of experience that are necessary. It means looking back to preliminaries that are necessary, instead of looking to consequences or results. Transcendental can be contrasted on the one hand to "transcendent," which is what is over and above or outside of experience, and on the other hand to "empirical," which is the content of the experience itself. The transcendental turn results in a fully reflexive philosophy. Here reflection means "thought about thought" about the world; we reflect when we think about the way in which we think. Kant holds that the a priori forms of both sensibility and understanding operate within the process of knowing. But only by "thought about thought" or reflection do we become aware of these forms. Not only do we become aware of them, but they must be organized in a systematic way from the most general to the most specific. The task of metaphysics as a science is to identify these forms, to justify their possibility, and to organize them into a system.

A second way to introduce the special Kantian meaning of transcendental is by means of a classification of propositions. Much earlier Aristotle, by an analysis of predication, made the distinction of substance from accidents and in this way gave the initial distinction for his system of categories. Kant calls one kind of proposition "empirical." These are synthetic a posteriori. The predicate adds to the subject in such propositions, which are therefore known by experience alone to be true or false. The natural sciences are largely composed of this sort of proposition, and that is why they are called "empirical" sciences. A second kind of proposition is called "analytic," or more technically, "analytic a priori." The subject and the predicate say the same thing. They are known to be true because of the meanings of the terms involved. There is no need of experience to confirm them. All definitions and tautologies are analytic. A third class of propositions is called synthetic a priori. These are what is meant when Kant uses the phrase "knowledge a priori." They are propositions that are significant about the world, namely, the predicate adds to the subject; but their truth does not come from experience, nor can they be falsified by experience.

The third class of propositions is controversial. Practically all philosophers subsequent to Kant have adopted a position for or against their legitimacy. Kant held that the identification, justification, and systematization of this third sort of proposition was the special work of metaphysics. This task made metaphysics distinct from empirical studies on the one hand and studies that made psuedo-claims to transcendent knowledge on the other. The system of a priori propositions is the science of metaphysics. It is a "science" not in the sense of being empirical, but in the sense of being organized and arranged so that one truth is connected to the others in a perfect system. The *Critique of Pure Reason* spells out this project; it tells how it is to be done. It was written to establish metaphysics on a firm ground. Such a foundation had in all times past been lacking. Part of the reason why it had been lacking is that the direction of thought had been wrong. Most earlier philosophers decided on a starting point and continued development of the further points of the system. Kant held that the main work of metaphysics was to look at the foundations of the starting point. Since the experiencing human self was the start, then metaphysics must look to the a priori conditions of the possibility of human experience.

Kant believed that certain helps are contributed to this project by the fields of mathematics and physics. They show the way to go. In addition, historically, Kant considered Newtonian physics, the synthetic a priori view of arithmetic, and Aristotelian logic as the final word. In each of these assumptions he was mistaken. Such mistakes as these, though embarrassing, do not upset the project that Kant set for himself.

The project of a systematic metaphysics in its general lines has a three-membered distinction as a basis. In the first place there is "sensibility," which is treated in the Transcendental Aesthetic. In this part Kant covers the a priori forms of sensibility which make possible our sense experience of the world. One part of this coverage is concerned with space. The second member of distinction is "understanding," which is covered in the Transcendental Analytic. Concepts are the a priori forms of understanding, and the table of concepts deduced systematically are the categories. These categories are the basic ways of thinking about things. They are forms of thought rather than modes of being. For example, "cause" and "substance" are two categories of relation. This means that to have experience of a world we must think of it as a plurality of causally interacting substances. The structured way of thinking about a world is necessary, and we are said to impose these categories on the world as necessary interpretive concepts. The third and final member of the distinction is "reason," which is treated in the Transcendental Dialectic. This part contains Kant's criticism of the faulty modes of thinking, that is, the illegitimate extension of thinking beyond the bounds of experience. For example, in this section one of Kant's tasks is to show that all proofs for the existence of a transcendent being or God are impossible.

The division into sensibility, understanding, and reason, along with the working out of the subdivisions under these headings, is what is called Kant's architectonic. It is the organizational scheme in which Kant structures his treatment of human experience. He is interested in showing the conditions of the possibility of human experience and its limits. The total listing and derivation of the forms of sensibility and the concepts of understanding are the conditions of the possibility of human experience. This is the positive section of the *Critique of Pure Reason*. The limits of human experience are set forth in the negative section. These limits are shown by a criterion of significance which separates what is beyond experience from what is within it. It is the device by which Kant fixes the limits of our knowledge to the empirical and the transcendental, and eliminates all transcendent claims. The way in which he fixes the limits of our knowledge is not in one fell swoop, as the Positivists later attempted to do with the verification principle, but piecemeal, bit by bit. He takes the various claims that are made for reason and its ideas, then shows the contradictions and impossibilities that result from transcendent claims made about the world, the self, and God. Such a criterion, if developed, will allow one to distinguish sense and nonsense, meaning and meaninglessness. Locke earlier talked about the limits of understanding. The felt need for setting such a limit comes from the amount of confusion thought to exist in philosophy. One explanation, which can be called the "remainder" theory, holds that philosophy has, because of its antiquity, become a storehouse. Like all old repositories it has been picked over from time to time, with the useful subjects removed and only odds and ends left. A general housecleaning is in order, but the need is for a principle of selection to distinguish the trash to be disposed of and the worthwhile to be salvaged.

For example, Kant explores the claim that is made to the effect that reason proves the existence of a transcendent being. His strategy in this case is to show that all arguments for God's existence, whether they be ontological, cosmological, or teleological, have at their root the ontological argument. He then goes on to show that the ontological argument is invalid. Consequently, all arguments for the existence of a transcendent being fail. Kant's basic objection to the ontological argument is, as we have seen, that "being" or "existence" is not a real predicate and hence adds nothing to the concept of something. One can never argue from a concept to the existence of what the concept signifies. This issue is one of the crucial metaphysical controversies. Philosophers are divided for and against on this issue. One interesting side-stepping of the controversy is by the "Transcendental Thomists," who lay claim to an intellectual intuition by which they hope to overcome the negative or agnostic aspects of the *Critique of Pure Reason.*

In his later years Kant extended his unique transcendental approach. In the *Critique of Practical Reason* he extended it to the field of morality. In the *Critique of Judgement* he extended it to aesthetics and teleology.

The overall results of Kant's work are of prime importance for the history of metaphysics. In terms of unity, Kant shows how metaphysics forms one system with no scattered parts; each section is related to all the others. Kant claims that he formulates the complete system of synthetic a priori propositions and hence that these and these alone are the totality of what metaphysics is about. Since the system gives the foundation of all thinking it fulfills the claim to basicness. His work is reflexive both in looking back at origins and in employing thought to discover the conditions of thinking. The transcendental approach which attempts to discover the conditions of the possibility of all thought and experience uses a special mode of argumentation. It is a way of discovering necessary presuppositions rather than necessary deductive consequences.

The revolution about the human person, begun by Descartes, reaches its climax in the philosophy of Kant in the following way. Philosophy is for all subsequent times human centered. No more is it possible to hold the view that the world is independent and objective. There is no such thing as the noumenal world that humans can know or speak of; there is no essence or thing in itself which philosophy investigates. Human knowledge is always phenomenal, in that it reveals at best the way things appear to us. Any claim to a one-to-one correspondence or likeness between experience and objects of experience cannot be established, simply because the second term of the claimed correspondence, objects of experience, are never known outside of experience. Without one of the two terms no correspondence can be talked about. Knowledge is always knowledge of a human subject; negatively phrased, the point is that the human subject is never separated out from the activity of knowing. Kant's philosophy, however, is not that all knowing is psychologically personal. He is not concerned with the psychology of human knowing which would be concerned with this human rather than another, with European consciousness as opposed to Oriental, or black consciousness, or female consciousness. Rather, his philosophy is about all human consciousness and experiencing without restriction, without any qualifying adjective.

## G. W. F. HEGEL

The philosophy of Kant fulfills many of the formal characteristics of a metaphysical system. But several crucial moves are still to be made. Hegel, for instance, gives several illustrations of key characteristics. This treatment will skip over the criticism he makes of Kant and what he finds as shortcomings in the Kantian system. The treatment is limited to the notion of dialectic and the integration of method with content; dialectic as applied to the human person will illustrate Hegel's philosophy.

Hegel's idea of philosophy is that it is the highest and the greatest activity of humans. It is heavily reflective and requires thought that is aware of itself. Hegel's style of writing requires the reader to be constantly reflexive. Literally "reflexive" means to bend back on oneself; here it means to be aware of what is happening, how it got there, and what the consequences are. The writing continually integrates itself. There is no split or separation of content and method. By "content" is understood the subject matter, the "what." By "method" is understood the way or mode of consideration, the "how." There is an integration, not a separation. The example of "dialectic" will help to show how this works. Frequently "dialectic" seems to say separate and divide. When one uses the idea of thesis-antithesis-synthesis, a separation or division seems implied. But these terms are not used by Hegel. They are mentioned only once in a side reference. Hegel more frequently describes dialectic as oppositions that are reconciled. In the first place any position generates its own opposition.

Nothing is final. Everything has an opposite. This is the nature of life. The key image is not a pendulum. Those who have this image in mind grasp only the first part, the oppositions. The point of dialectic is that things and events are not stable but fluid, in constant change. Secondly, there is the reconciliation of opposites. Oppositions must be overcome. They are brought together not by compromise in which part of each is taken, but in such a way that each entirely is present; there is no loss. This is a big claim. How can Hegel deliver what the claim promises? Dialectic must get both as they are in opposition and bring them together completely. Full flexibility of mind is needed. We must be open to new alternatives and not cancel things out, but rather integrate them. Consider some concrete representations. A point will not do as an explanation of dialectic because it indicates stability. Nor will a line do, whether straight or wavy, because the last part never integrates the first part. The pendulum has already been rejected because it is oscillating repetition. Hegel himself uses the image of a circle as as illustration. But from his own descriptions it is better to use a spiral or a spring which is ever returning but at a new level.

Philosophy for Hegel calls for an integration of content and method; it is also dialectical. How can this be? Some speak of philosophy as content. For example, in the question: What is so-and-so's philosophy? the "what" asks for a list of specifications. But such a view is, according to Hegel, inadequate. Rather, one must ask for the content/method. The slash indicates that the two notions cannot be separated or put side by side as different. On the other hand some speak of dialectic as method. They might ask, What method is used? The word "used" indicates an activity, a process, as if it were separate from results or what comes about. This view is likewise, according to Hegel, incorrect. The question should not ask for the activity or the mode of procedure alone, but rather the activity and the procedure should be one with the content. As unclear as this may sound, the point that Hegel is trying to make calls for a rearrangement of our viewpoint. Whereas we might be accustomed to make some divisions and identifications, he is trying to shift the view around.

Hegel's approach is to raise a question about a starting point in philosophy. Is it mediate? It is not this, because as such it would be objective and give only content. Is it immediate? It is not this, because such would be subjective and be exempt from method and logic. Our conclusion might be that there is no starting point. Hegel suggests we rather try a third alternative. The starting point is both mediate and immediate. This unites both the content and the method, the principle and the form. Pure being or being in general on the one hand and nothing on the other are a unity. He speaks of non-being which is being, and being which is non-being. He tells us that these should be interpreted not as contradictions but as progressive development. Take the example of life: First there is the bud, then the blossom, and finally the fruit; together these are an organic unity. But analytically one could take these as a series of separations and oppositions. Each subsequent stage could be taken as an opposition to what it succeeds, and it can be considered to come about only by cancelling out the previous stage. But we do not take living things analytically but rather as organic unities. They are not a series of separations and oppositions that work by cancellation. The clue must be taken from a view that we already have of life. The life of the mind should be regarded as an organic unity. It is a process of reconciliation of oppositions. This is dialectic. This is the integration of method and content.

So far the development of Hegel's philosophy has been theoretical. It started from a simple problem about "beginning" in philosophy. There were some abstract considerations about difficulties encountered and a theoretical treatment of the way out of the difficulties. The organic unity of life is the key. A hint was taken from biology, and this suggests an application to theoretical philosophy about "being," about "consciousness."

We can also see Hegel's theory at work in a description of human interrelationships. There is a passage from *The Phenomenology of Spirit* about lordship and bondage which has had influence on some of the Existentialists, especially Sartre. In this passage Hegel points out that self-consciousness means independence and dominance. But these are relative concepts. We are independent only when there is the other and the other is dependent. There is dominance only when there is the other and the other is dominated. In Hegel's terms, lord is lord only with bondsman as bondsman. But if this is true, then the one who is independent is also dependent, because he needs others who are dependent. Likwise the dependent is independent when he discovers that he is needed by the one who is independent. Thus independence is dependence and dependence is independence. Neither is alone. Neither is what it is without including its opposite. For this opposition a reconciliation is needed. It is difficult to achieve. If there is a reconciliation, then it is perhaps momentary because it is the nature of life to be continually changing.

The process is akin to that of mirroring. One reflects to another and at the same time records the reflection as it is received in the other. One who sees himself as another sees him, needs the other's perception for self-perception. In addition this means that he needs the other. The other's perception of oneself changes one's self-perception. This change in self-perception changes myself, and if the other perceives this change in me, then his perception of me is changed from what it was before. This is ongoing; there is no stop. Each stage works out of a prior stage which it follows and by which it is influenced. Consciousness preserves both but is not fixed to either. Its nature is the same as that of life—to be ongoing and successive.

Hegel illustrates "process" in philosophy. A system should be open to incorporation of further developments. Hegel's writings exhibit the characteristic of unity in an unusual way—by doing what he is talking about, by both informing and illustrating at the same time. Finally, he illustrates a grasp of reflexiveness, not only by thinking about thought, but also by challenging the reader to become totally aware that the process of thinking and the reality of oneself are intertwined.

Begins process philosophy.
Whole of World one big thought.

# IV
# THE CONTEMPORARIES

One prominent feature of the modern period in philosophy is variety in both types of systems and viewpoints. A fragmentation has occurred in philosophy, and there are multiple views leading in many different directions. This multiplicity is in some ways overwhelming, and it is difficult to detect any unity of direction or growth. Some principles of organization are needed to help bring the diversity into some sort of unity. The diffusion that occurred is perhaps more understandable if it is seen first of all as a consequence of the conception of an open universe that developed out of Renaissance science. It was no longer appropriate to restrict philosophy to a closed world; rather, new and multiple possibilities were constantly surfacing. A second factor encouraging diffusion was the fact that the new writings in philosophy were composed outside the confines of the schools. There was no fixed curriculum to direct or restrict the choice of subject matter or treatment.

In addition to this diffusion of direction, another noteworthy feature of the modern period is the autonomy of philosophy. Frequently this autonomy is presented from the viewpoint that areas or fields of study separated from philosophy. Here, the proposal is that philosophy can be viewed as having become autonomous from other fields of study. First, there is the separation from religion and theology. The area of the transcendent, or what is over and above experience, is no longer regarded as the principal nor even the proper area of concern for philosophy. Then, there is the separation from the natural sciences. What is empirical, the content of what is gained from or provable by experience, is the concern of the natural sciences and not a matter for philosophy. The proper area of concern for philosophy is, with increasing agreement, considered to be the reflexive, or what is called by Kant the transcendental. The presuppositions or the necessary assumptions of other studies are studied in philosophy. With this focus philosophy concentrates on what is basic; it studies fundamentals, the concepts and principles that underlie other studies. In this viewpoint philosophy retains a connection with the older tradition that it is the study of all things, but in a special way, namely, that it studies the underlying bases of other areas of studies. In addition philosophy is "reflexive" in the sense that its views must be self-applicable; they must be tested for consistency. At this point the connection of philosophy and logic is closest.

Philosophy's growing autonomy in the modern period helped to narrow its scope. It was not the study of everything in any way. Its main focus came to be the bases or fundamentals of a world which is open and all-encompassing. Although, in part, the older tradition in philosophy remains alive, it is no longer the central direction. The older tradition consisted in the study of a really existing independent world. By intent it worked to discover the essence or nature of things. Most frequently it elaborated theories of being, or substance, or some other one central feature. One of the most notable outcomes of the modern period in philosophy is that it has focused on analyzing the foundational concepts and principles needed in empirical studies.

In the contemporary period, which is the subject of this chapter, the multiplicity of viewpoints and systems is even more noticeable than in the modern period. The volume of philosophy produced intensifies the problems of selecting representative figures and identifying trends. The observation has been made that more philosophy has been written in this period than in any of the others; "more" is here understood both in terms of variety of viewpoints and in regard to volume of what is published. The point is that it is even more difficult to have some unity of viewpoint or discover some connecting principles for this, the contemporary period.

But difficulties do not make the situation hopeless. For example, much of what is produced in books and journals today are analyses or criticisms of what has been done before. Also, much is connected to some of the previous developments by way of extension or reversal. The time period for this chapter is the twentieth century. With few exceptions it will deal with works written after 1900. Within this restriction of time only a few philosophers who have been leaders or have set trends in the development of philosophy have been selected for treatment.

Any understanding of developments and directions, any assessments that are made of mistakes and blindnesses, are risky. The overview taken here is pretentious and has its own set of dangers. The view of somewhat Olympian in the sense of being handed down from the heights of Mount Olympus. It is hoped that an overview can be taken and comparisons made because we are in a sense outside of and once removed from the scene. The analogy has been phrased that we are pygmies who stand on the shoulders of giants. We profit by what others have done. Their work has brought our own thinking along further and faster. We do not have to repeat the same labored efforts, but we do have to rethink what others have made possible for us to do more quickly and with a greater sense of origins and directions.

The giants for philosophy in the contemporary period are many. In particular Hume, Kant, and Hegel have had great influence on those who write philosophy in the twentieth century. In the first place, in the case of metaphysics, Hume is overwhelmingly negative and skeptical of all speculation and system building in philosophy. He is a destructive critic and consciously so. Then there is Kant, who by intention and execution set the groundwork for systematic metaphysics. He was also a critic who pointed out the basic flaws of his predecessors. A final influence of great importance is Hegel, who as a philosopher is overwhelmingly positive and a practitioner of speculation. He seems to recognize no problems or limitations to doing philosophy on the grand scale. Even though these philosophers are very different among themselves, they are yet major influences on philosophy of the contemporary period. It is possible to say that earlier trends merge into them and the twentieth century in philosophy comes out of them. There is little done today in philosophy that does not relate to one or all of them.

## BERTRAND RUSSELL

Hume's skepticism is in some ways related to the way in which he analyzes language. The restrictions placed on knowing are related to a way of classifying propositions. Such analyses of language neither originate with nor conclude with Hume. Aristotle used subject/predicate analysis as one of the arguments for substance/attribute metaphysics. Kant used classification of kinds of propositions as groupings of ways to study the world. This technique becomes explicit and dominant in the twentieth century. A decisive part in establishing language analysis is played by Bertrand Russell and the doctrine of logical atomism. Russell is not a member of the movement known as "linguistic analysis"; in many ways he was an opponent of some of the individual practitioners within the movement. Yet Russell prepared the way. In addition to extensive work in mathematics and logic, he related this work to the subject of language. Russell studies the structure of language as a way to discover what there is, what exists, which is a way of establishing a metaphysics or ontology. Logic understood as the analysis of the structure of language and the search for a perfect language becomes the central point of metaphysics. It was not logic understood in the older sense, but logic with the developments of Peano, Boole, and others.

It may help to clarify the relation of metaphysics or ontology on the one hand to language or logic on the other by reviewing a few things about Kant. Kant's philosophy relates mind and world in a unique way. The relation is such that structure of mind dictates and is part of the structure of the world. There cannot be a world as such or experience as such because the world to be a world or experience to be experience must be organized, structured, arranged. This organizing, structuring, arranging is a work of the mind. Only when we are fully reflexive in our thinking can we go back over our experience and pick out the mental contribution which gives form to, organizes, structures, or arranges our experience. The mental structures for Kant are the forms of sensibility or space and time, and the concepts of understanding or categories. Kant talks about forms, thoughts, ideas, concepts, all of which are mental. Yet in one sense, what is mental is one's own or private to oneself. But if Kant claims to study *all* human experience with no exception, then these claims must extend to what is beyond only our own, i.e., the mental. One thing that is objectively available equally to all is language. It is not difficult to make a change in Kant's doctrine so that the analysis is of the structures of the language which we use to express our thoughts about the world. The attention paid to language rather than thought introduces the note of publicness into the analysis. A note of caution about the exposition used here. The model behind this mode of exposition is a direct line: language—thought—world. The linear model falsifies one of the main points which Kant was making. The Kantian move in philosophy is to show how the last relation [thought—world] is never separate or successive.

Rather, the model is $\begin{bmatrix}\text{WORLD}\\ \text{thought}\end{bmatrix}$

Next, the suggestion of the change for the Kantian model is to substitute "language" for "thought."

The model then becomes $\begin{bmatrix}\text{WORLD}\\ \text{language}\end{bmatrix}$

This latter can be called a "linguistic Kantianism." It holds that our world, or experience, is what it is because of the structures or forms of the language we have. This is not in the sense of English, French, Chinese, etc., but language in the sense of the root structures of what we say and/or write that are general and common to every particular natural language. This viewpoint can be named "linguistic Kantianism" and more will be said about it, especially in the chapter on "Projections."

Bertrand Russell was not a Kantian, and he did not hold the doctrine here called linguistic Kantianism. He did play a decisive part in preparation for this doctrine. It was logical atomism, not in its specifics, but in orientation and assumptions which prepared the way for the dominance of language analysis as one of the important directions of contemporary philosophy.

The specifics of logical atomism show it to be a metaphysical doctrine. It proposes to tell us what there is in the world and what it is like. Logical atomism holds that the world in its ultimate structure is composed of "facts." Things, or particulars of the world, are complex. The task of analysis is to discover the ultimate simples. Particulars of the world have plural qualities and relations. The nonreducible properties and relations of the particulars of the world are called "facts." When they are nonreducible and ultimately simple they are called "atomic facts". For example, x can be red, round, spongy, lying on the floor, to my north, etc. To "say" a fact is to use language which is expressible in propositions. The words that make up propositions are simple if they are not further reducible. Such words would be "red" and others like it. Since these words name qualities, they are known as simple predicates. The other kinds of simple words for particulars of the world are proper names, each of which picks out one specific in the world, for example, "this" when referring to one and only one item, or "Socrates" as said of the Greek philosopher, teacher of Plato. The combination of a proper name and a simple predicate, for example, "This is red," is an atomic proposition. These simplest or atomic propositions name atomic facts. Atomic facts are what make atomic propositions true.

Out of atomic propositions it is possible to construct more complex ones which are called molecular propositions. The construction is done by use of the laws of truth-functional logic, that is, by using the laws governing the use of truth-functional connectives such as "and," "or," etc. These molecular propositions are "truth-functions" of atomic propositions; their truth or falsity is dependent solely upon the atomic propositions of which they are constructed. Though there are molecular propositions, there are no molecular facts, only atomic facts.

The explanation developed here of Russell's version of logical atomism has built up from atomic facts to molecular propositions. Analysis is actually the other way around. Russell holds that the language we use and anyone's language in its complexities can be analyzed or broken down into its simples of atomic propositions. This is the syntax of a perfect language. Its syntactic structure is atomic, and its complexities are constructs which use the laws of truth-functional logic. Russell assumed this was true of the language of day-to-day usage. Moreover, any language whatever, provided its imperfections were removed, would analyze out into this skeleton as it were or essence of language.

Russell's basic move of going from the structure of language to the structure of the world is not entirely new. Aristotle has as one of the roots of his substance/attribute metaphysics the subject/predicate structure of language. But Russell holds that Aristotle uses an incomplete logic. It is possible to relate Aristotle and Russell in the following way: If language has a subject/predicate structure then metaphysics can be substance/attribute. And one of Aristotle's arguments for his metaphysics proceeds from the fact of the subject/predicate language structure. But if the subject/predicate structure of language is not the only structure of language or, what is more, is not the basic structure of language, then substance is not the main metaphysical doctrine or, even more strongly, the metaphysical doctrine of substance is misconceived. Russell argues that the world is composed not only of particulars and qualities but also of relations. It is these latter, "relations" and the logic of relations, that show in the first place the insufficiency of Aristotelian logic and consequently why such a metaphysics is no longer viable.

However different they may be, both Russell and Aristotle operate with at least one similar assumption: there is a parallel between the ontological structure of reality and the logical structure of sentences. For Aristotle it is at best only implicit and its use is casual and partial, but for Russell it is a central feature of his metaphysics and so explicit that it might be better to call it a principle rather than an assumption. Russell regards sentences as pictures of reality. The simplest sentences depict the non-reducible items of experience. This later tendency to search for simples is not from Aristotle but is more probably Russell's inheritance from the British empiricists Locke, Berkeley, and Hume. The terminus of analysis is in what is theoretically indispensable for a logically perfect language.

Many features of the doctrine of logical atomism are objectionable. Not the least of these objections would be to either of the previously mentioned assumptions. Some critics are unable to accept the isomorphism of language and the world; others object to the reduction to simples as basic. There are even more problems. Russell himself found that he could not avoid a commitment to general facts or negative facts which others found to be incompatible with the demands of parsimony. There are also three paradoxical results of Russell's exposition. Though all his arguments are rooted in and come out of a view of language, it is strange that he considers language as only propositional; that he would forget that there were more functions and uses of language than those of truth and falsity is a serious lapse. Secondly, with Russell it now becomes a major focus in philosophy to deliver an adequate theory of meaning, but Russell's own fact ontology as so developed is a result of a confusion of meaning with reference. Finally, there is the suicidal aspect of logical atomism. As a philosophical doctrine it limits the meaningful to the assertion of facts. But the theory does not state facts; rather it talks at least in part about the relation of facts and the world. According to the theory, such talk about facts, since it is not the assertion of facts, is outside the realm of the sayable and the meaningful. Thus the theory by its own principles is meaningless.

One of the legacies for the twentieth century from Bertrand Russell's work in philosophy is the concentration on the study of the structure of language. One direction which this takes is that of the construction of artificial languages. In this sense Carnap is one of the main heirs of the work initiated by Russell. Others argue that a natural language system, or what is called ordinary language, is the area on which to concentrate. A major reason advanced for study of ordinary over artificial languages is that we start with what is given or the language system into which we are born; it is only secondarily and derivatively that a formal language can be constructed. Whichever direction one takes, what is called the analytic movement in philosophy which has been predominant in English-speaking countries is in good part the result of Russell's writings.

## MARTIN HEIDEGGER

Martin Heidegger, a primary figure in contemporary philosophy, represents a philosophical tradition quite different from that of Russell. Some speak of a split in twentieth-century philosophy; on the one hand there is the Continental classical orientation, and on the other hand there is the Anglo-American empirical tradition. This is a somewhat crude and oversimplified distinction; yet it has some value. The one direction and set of interests is molded by the humanities, the arts, and religion, whereas the second has its tone and animation from the natural sciences, mathematics, and logic. Heidegger, with reservations and qualifications, may be said to belong to the Continental tradition and has been considerably influenced by Hegel. He has revived in his philosophy the classical question of "being." Central to the study of metaphysics is the issue, "What is being?"

Heidegger is critical of what has happened in Western philosophy since the time of Plato. There has been a forgetfulness of being. The study of "beings" (with a small 'b' and an 's') has gotten in the way of or replaced the study of "Being" (with a large 'B' and no 's'). "Being," though the most general of all concepts, is neither attained nor identified without its own special problems. The diverse interpretations are an indication of the problems attached to it. One of the difficulties about Being is that it cannot be defined or identified in any of the traditional ways. In the first place there is nothing else that is simpler or more basic by which it can be identified or coordinated. A more serious problem is that it cannot be dealt with from outside. There is nothing more general nor is there any standpoint outside. One cannot as in most other investigations assume a distinction of investigator and investigated. On the other hand, the inquiry is not asking about a being and therefore just any being will not do; it is about nothing less than Being itself.

Heidegger's approach in the midst of this difficulty is to start the search from a being, and this being has to include in the quest its own being. There is only one being that can meet this requirement—the human being. A human is the only being who is a questioner, and the asking of the question involves the questioner in the question. The human is tied into the inquiry about Being in the special sense that the human both changes the inquiry because part of the data is not only that there are beings but that one of them inquires about Being. The human is changed by the inquiry because the realization of the difference from other beings and the practice of this mode of thinking intensifies human uniqueness among beings. The investigation of the human reality, of *Dasein* as Heidegger calls it, is both the starting point and the main focus of the investigation. Though Heidegger never changed his thinking that *Dasein* was the privileged starting point, he has had second thoughts about its adequacy in overcoming the difficulties of attaining Being rather than beings.

In addition to the difficulties of starting point and definition of Being, Heidegger talks about the difficulty caused by the common assumption that Being is the totality of what is. The assumed identification of being and existence leaves out any consideration of the "ground" of what is. Other than existence, there is only nothing that can function as the ground of what is. Heidegger explains that "nothing" is an integral part of any study of Being. The introduction of nothing is not conceptual but experiential. Heidegger's point is not that the limits of sense are shown by engaging in nonsense. It is not that we must go beyond the limits and foundations in order to understand these limits, or try out the meaningless to get the totality of meaning. Heidegger's claim is that "nothing" along with "what is" makes up Being. The proof for the inclusion of nothing is not conceptual but experiential. It consists in a showing of nothing, not in the act of negation, but in fundamental human experience. The key mood of "dread" (Angst) brings a human, in experience, face to face with Nothing. This experience of Nothing makes possible an understanding of "what is," and in turn the full metaphysics of Being becomes possible.

The introduction of the discussion of "nothing" has resulted in many reactions against Heidegger's philosophy. There are the superficial criticisms of Ayer, who with tongue in cheek allows that "being" for all its problems is backed in our dictionaries by the verb "to be," but protests that "nothing" has no equivalent verb "to noth." Carnap, with seriousness, uses the phrase from Heidegger, "Das Nichts nichtet," as a prime example of a philosopher's misuse of language ending as nonsense. The use of "das" makes "Nothing" into a substantive. Carnap points out that Heidegger seems not to notice that "nothing" as a substantive makes it something and no longer nothing. But an even greater piece of nonsense is that for Heidegger "Nothing" is not only a substantive but it carries on an activity of "nihilation."

In Heidegger's defense the tradition of Parmenides can be recalled. It was in pre-Socratic philosophy that the two paths of being and non-being were set out. Parmenides chose the first because of the inexpressibility of the second. Perhaps recognizing this Heidegger does not attempt to conceptualize "nothing," a procedure by which it would be made into a "something" at least for thought. His claim is not so strong in that regard; but the claim is stronger in another way, in that nothing is revealed in a fundamental human experience of dread. A claim made in this way is protected in that it can be affirmed or denied only by each one of himself.

Heidegger in our day revives the classic question of being with a new twist. For him it is Being in the most general sense as grounded in or arising from its limits of Nothing. In addition, some insight is thrown on topics that are so general as to include both the topic and the one who raises the topic. Generality that becomes self-inclusive calls with it the characteristic of consistency. The only method that can handle this will be reflexive. There is no separation of object and method. It is true to say both that we discover the object by using the method and also that we discover the method by using it in reference to the object. All this we become aware of by knowing what we are doing when we are doing it.

## ALFRED NORTH WHITEHEAD

Alfred North Whitehead is perhaps the only one in the history of Western philosophy not only to have a clear conception of a metaphysical system of philosophy but also to have worked through with discipline and rigor the details of the system. Whitehead is here selected for treatment not only because of the outline of the project of a metaphysical system but especially for its detailed accomplishment. His career had its beginnings in mathematics. In collaboration with Bertrand Russell he produced the major initiator work in mathematics and logic of the twentieth century: *Principia Mathematica*. There are some similarities in the philosophical systems of Russell and Whitehead. The world is made up of "facts" for Russell and "events" for Whitehead; both of these views stand in opposition to a "thing" or "substance" view of reality. Again, these "facts" or "events" are the minimals or smallest items out of which or in light of which all else is made up and understood. Probably the major difference between the two is their views on language. For Russell a study of the structure of language is the royal road into metaphysics. On the contrary, for Whitehead, language follows after metaphysics, and words can be altered or changed because of the demands of metaphysical construction; it is to be hoped that language can become an ever more adequate vehicle of metaphysical thinking.

Whitehead's general orientation in philosophy, other than speculative or metaphysical, can best be characterized by the word "process." The system of process he has constructed has time as a dynamic factor built in as opposed to timeless, static viewpoints. He is attempting to account for the manifold interrelations of past and present with the future left open. The terminology is novel and exclusively his. It takes a long time and a lot of familiarity to enter thoroughly into his philosophy.

Here the exposition of Whitehead's contribution will be limited to some of the generalities of his ideas about philosophy and some of the specifics of the system, in order to show in some detail that it is a process philosophy. Whitehead uses the terms speculative philosophy and metaphysics interchangeably. His system allows for the demands of both reason and experience. Reason is required by the coherence or interrelation of the fundamental ideas as opposed to their isolation. In addition, reason asks for adherence to logic in the sense that the basic concepts be consistent among themselves. These requirements of reason show a relation to Hegel and the doctrine of internal relations, which holds that everything is connected to everything else and makes a difference for it. However, Whitehead rejected a somewhat standard doctrine of rationalism to the effect that basics of a system be clear and distinct and the rest be deducible from these. In opposition, Whitehead holds to the continual clarification and perfectibility of any part, even foundational, of his system. Besides reason there are also some demands made by experience on the system. Not only the origins of the system but also the test of it is found in experience. The system must apply to our experience, and the system must be able to accommodate whatever is experienced. The actual world and ourselves are both the source and the justification of our thought.

The very same characterization of the sort of philosophy that Whitehead considers legitimate is found in the treatment of method. The primary method of philosophy is considered to be "descriptive generalization." The operative word in this phrase is "generalization" in the sense that truths that philosophy seeks are to be broad and far-reaching. But both the origin and object of these generalizations are to be the specifics of daily life. Whitehead uses the picture of the flight of an airplane to help our understanding. Both the take-off and the landing are the data of solid earth; but the flight is the series of wide views that occur between but are connected to both beginnings and endings. Part of the difference between philosophy and the natural sciences is the wider scope of philosophical generalizations. In both cases, however, the generalizations are working hypotheses subject to

testing, revision, reformulation, or even rejection. The test for a philosophical system is progress, not finality. The system must remain open for revision and alteration; it is never closed or finished.

Whitehead sketches an attractive view of a philosophical system. It is a logical scheme that is to interpret experience, yet is tentative and open to revision. The basic concept of Whitehead's metaphysical system is the "actual entity," or, what is generally equivalent, the "actual occasion." These "entities" or "occasions" are what is "really real," that of which the world is made up. They are the locus of agency, the fullness of being. Neither the happening nor what happens is apart from or behind actual entities. They are agency, process, the being, the becoming of the world. They are not any sort of entity that can be recognized by common sense or ordinary observation. The actual entity is microscopic or atomic only in that it is the minimal of experience, but it is not sense observable even with supplementation by instruments. It does not endure in time but perishes the moment it becomes. It is the "drop" of experience but not separated out and independent from other entities. All actual entities are related and interdependent. They are immortal in that each enters into all subsequent actual entities.

The conception of "prehension" explains the relatedness and interdependence of actual entities. The actual entity brings together in concrete unity the diverse elements by way of a prehension. The prehension is the grasping or absorbing of the total field that goes to make up an actual entity. There are various kinds of prehensions in the formation of the concrete unity of a given actual entity. The attainment of the internal form of the entity is called satisfaction. The entity, having attained satisfaction, perishes and in turn is prehended by later actual entities. This progression of prehension, satisfaction, perishing, and being prehended shows the process, the relatedness, and the immortality of an actual entity. The experiences, the objects of common sense and ordinary experience, are technically "nexūs" or societies or organized groupings of actual entities.

The concrescence, which is the process of formation of the

actual entity as the minimal item from which the events of the world are made up, presupposes three formative elements. These three key concepts are creativity, eternal objects, and God. "Creativity" is the principle of novelty. Each actual entity is novel or diverse from the many others which it prehends or the manyness of the others into which it is prehended. The newness of the specific concreteness of any given actual entity is due to creativity. It is this creativity that Whitehead designates, together with the equally basic notions of "one" and "many," the "category of the ultimate." Creativity is ultimate in the sense that it is both the common ground of all actualities and also the individualization of each actuality. The creativity is not a thing or event but a principle of the concrete togetherness and novelty of each actual entity.

"Eternal objects" are a second formative element of Whitehead's system. They are timeless ideas which supply permanence to ceaseless flux. Eternal objects can be considered counterparts to be contrasted to the individuality and uniqueness of actual entities. They are alternatively called "pure potentials" or "forms of definiteness" by Whitehead. They are prehended conceptually as opposed to the physical prehension of past actual entities. The determinate form of a specific actual entity is the result of its own creative decision as to which eternal objects will be allowed to ingress into its concrescence.

"God" is the third formative element. Whitehead's doctrine about God is both integral and essential to the total completeness of the system. The key function of God is to relate the permanent but possible ideals to the flux of actual entities. The dual nature of God, which is both primordial and consequent, is not only an unusual aspect of Whitehead's doctrine of God but also that by which actual entities and eternal objects are bound into one coherent system. In his primordial nature God prehends all eternal objects; in his consequent nature he prehends all actual entities. The primordial nature is conceptual and static, whereas the consequent nature is conscious and dynamic. The consequent nature is that by which God is with the world; it is in process prehending all actual entities. The objective immortality of each concrescing and perishing actual entity is assured because of the consequent nature of God.

The three formative elements in their interaction are mutually interdependent; the universe of actual entities emerges from their interaction. One writer compares the connection to the fuel, the pistons, and the sparking device needed to result in an operating internal combustion engine. There is no dynamic system if any one of the three is lacking. "Process" or "becoming" characterizes Whitehead's system, but "change" or "motion" does not. The fundamental entities in Whitehead's system do not change; they "become." Change speaks of a series of differences in the same thing; in somewhat the same sense "motion" denotes change of position. But for Whitehead the becoming of an actual entity is its perishing. Further, its perishing brings about its objective immortality, because then it becomes data for all subsequent entities. "Process" is the term used to describe the dynamic, continual, ongoing character of his system.

Some of the detail as included here indicates how intricate Whitehead's system is and how tightly the fundamental notions are interconnected. Many other details and subdivisions have been unmentioned. New terminology was introduced in this exposition as quickly as possible to enable the construction of sentences consisting almost entirely of Whitehead's own philosophical vocabulary. But it is even more important to realize how process can be integrated into a system of philosophy. In the first place Whitehead is attempting to have his reader undergo a process. We are asked to revise our view of the world; our thinking is to undergo a development. An even more important "process" is to occur in relation to language. In Whitehead's view, language is to be changed and even created so that it becomes ever more adequate to express our conceptions and the demands of the system. But most of all, process is so fundamental that not even the system is exempt from its demands. A system of philosophy can never be closed but must remain open for revision, addition, and alteration. Not only its main characterization but also the test of any system of philosophy, Whitehead holds, is not finality but progress. A system of metaphysics is to be measured by how much more adequate, how much further advanced, are the descriptive generalizations that it generates.

## WILLARD VAN ORMAN QUINE

The final representative choice for a contemporary figure in philosophy is an American, Willard Van Orman Quine. He shares some connection with both Russell and Whitehead. This connection is by way of the pioneering logical-mathematical work of the twentieth century: *Principia Mathematica*. One of Quine's earliest works is a technical logical work which he calls "closely allied" to the system of the *Principia* of Russell and Whitehead. Oddly enough, Quine is in no way related to the specifically philosophical work of either Russell or Whitehead as we have presented them here. In his writings he shows no influence of or affinity to either logical atomism or process philosophy.

Quine has done important original work in logic; this is logic understood both in the narrow sense of the technical systematic study of the forms of inference and also in the wider sense of the implications for and the relation to language. He has also been influential in the field of epistemology by directing a challenge to the rigidity of the analytic/synthetic distinction. The central point of the treatment here is going to be Quine's interest in "ontology" and the relation that language has to this area.

"Ontology" is a term that began to be widely used in the seventeenth century. Some use it interchangeably with metaphysics. Others, probably the greater number, use it as a subdivision of metaphysics. Specifically, they understand it as concentrating on the study of being or the question of existence in its most general sense but excluding more particular questions about God, the world, or humans. Quine understands ontology in this latter sense of the study of "what there is." The special way he has of phrasing his interest in ontology is to study the commitments of a given theory. He is interested in bringing out the existence of the entities to which a theory commits the one who holds it. For example, Russell points out that relations are a special sort of entity whose existence must be acknowledged; Whitehead holds to the existence of, among other things, eternal objects; Heidegger proposes (perhaps?) the existence of nothing. One's ontology is expressible in terms of the value of the variables that are needed to state a given theory. "Variable" here is a conception taken from logic. One of the key distinctions in logic is between constants and variables. "Constants" are the connectives; they stay the same and function in preset ways. "Variables" are those parts of sentences that are changing, and they carry the content of the proposition. The value of a variable is what that variable stands for in a given instance; this is what exists; it is the value of the variable to which we attribute "to be." It is in this sense that Quine's slogan is to be understood: " 'to be' is to be the value of a variable." Any theory needs a specific set of variables in order to be expressed; existence must be attributed to the values of these variables. More in Quine's sort of phrasing: we have to admit the existence of that range of entities for which names could occur as values for those variables without which we could not state a given theory. This is a logical test for the existence commitments in a given theory. To be able to quantify over a given variable that is necessary to state a theory is to commit one who holds such a theory to that sort of existence; the total number of the sorts of existences that a theory commits one to constitutes its ontology.

So far we have a test for the ontology of any given theory. But this says nothing about any given ontology; nor does it allow us to choose or advocate one ontology rather than another. Quine himself prefers nominalistic ontologies to platonistic ones. This means that he opts for "poor" or "thin" ontologies which admit the fewest possible number of existences. Specifically, he makes his decisions in light of two further principles. They are "scientific realism" and "the principle of parsimony." "Scientific realism" is the position that whatever science says is true; whatever science says exists, is. This commits one to the present state of scientific research and development at the given time. It is not a final commitment to a specific set of entities but changes with the status of the science of the day. The "principle of parsimony," also called colloquially "Ockham's razor," literally is phrased that "entities are not to be multiplied without necessity." This means that the fewest number of entities needed to explain a theory are to be preferred over any other explanation. Connecting Quine's two principles, one can explain his ontology as the fewest possible number of types of existences needed to explain the science of our day.

The ontology that Quine advocates is open-ended in the sense that there is no definitive finality at any given time. The older conception of metaphysics as a deductively certain theory that is good for all times and excludes all alternative theories is rejected. But Quine's ontology is even more open in light of a further special and unique doctrine: the indeterminacy of translation. According to this doctrine the same set of facts admits of at least several incompatible interpretation schemes. In other words, even though there is no factual disagreement, alternative theoretical arrangements are still possible. One consequence is that theoretical differences that are irreconcilable on a factual level are entirely possible. They are irreconcilable because there is no way of adjudicating the differences. If there is a point for metaphysics it is that an openness about theories must always exist. We can study about various theories, but there always will be a variety of them with no way of reaching a definitive conclusion about one over the others. This of course does not say that any theory is equally acceptable; some theories are fallacious, some are out of style, etc. But the point is that no one is definite and final.

Along with this point about the openness we must preserve regarding metaphysical or ontological theories, Quine brings out several other important points about language in relationship to the conduct of philosophy. The most general point is that language is related to logic so that the way into the structure of language is analyzed by way of logic and the techniques developed there. Again, it is by way of analysis of a given language system that one can construct the ontology lying at the base of that system. Quine's most important point is that however diverse ontologies may be, yet the common matters that can be talked about, be they ever so trivial, such as the time of day or the weather, show that language is the source area of agreement. Conversely, the divergences and disagreements can be mapped out according to the linguistic expressions admissible according to a given system. The philosophy of language and philosophy are deeply intertwined.

# V
# OBJECTIONS

The last four chapters traced metaphysics and metaphysical systems through the history of Western philosophy from the Greeks of several centuries B.C. to roughly our own time. The history of metaphysics has not been simple or harmonious. Not only are there objections to the individual arguments used by philosophers, such as the difficulties with the individual premises of the ontological argument of Anselm, but there are also more general objections to the entire position taken by a philosopher, for example the difficulty with the position of a dualistic view of a human being taken by Descartes.

This chapter attempts to gather some of the more significant objections that are made about metaphysics. In some cases the objections are about individual arguments; in other cases they may be about a metaphysical position or system; but it is especially the objections about metaphysics in general that must be examined. It is not so much the specific objection but rather the point being made that allows us to generalize and compare similarities rather than leave the objections as individual and random. The attempt will be made to pick out common flaws that may have occurred. There are several advantages to doing this. The first is that a study of objections will help us to understand the claims that are made. This can clarify our appreciation of a viewpoint even if it is not our own, but alien and foreign. Secondly, the evaluation of arguments and objections is an exercise that can increase our skills in doing philosophy. We will be actively engaging in the process of argumentation and evaluation by defending or refuting various metaphysical positions and systems. Thirdly, it is important to make the problems, objections, and failures instructive. Constructive use of the objections can indicate directions and projections for future metaphysical systems. A separate chapter is devoted to this theme. In addition, some specific figures in the history of philosophy associated with the label "anti-metaphysical" will be studied, namely: Hume, Kant, Carnap, and Lazerowitz.

Before discussing some objections to metaphysics in general and some individuals called anti-metaphysical, we need to make several clarifications about the presentation in these pages. The approach has not been descriptive, not neutral, not without a viewpoint. As a first example, consider the model which was proposed in the Introduction. It listed the formal characteristics for any metaphysical system. This is an ideal construct. It can be used as tool; in such case it can be an extension of our own abilities. Physical tools like the wheel assist movement over a distance, and the lever multiplies our ability to pry and lift. The model of a metaphysical system as a tool gives an extension of degree and intensity to the ability that is already there. If the model used as a tool is helpful, it can be a key to open up writings, to ask of them some major questions, and it can be a probe to locate the important issues. But conversely, it can happen that a model becomes harmful. It can be a procrustean bed. The mythical character Procrustes had an iron bed to accommodate all visitors. It was one size, but it fit everyone; if the visitor was short he was stretched, if too long he had his extremities chopped off so he could fit in the bed. A model can be harmful if it chops or mutilates what is to be left alone or understood in its own right. The point is that a model can be helpful or harmful; it can have its advantages or disadvantages. In any case, the model does not do the work but is an extension of our abilities that can help to take us along further and faster. It is evaluative, serving to check, to measure, to raise the quality of our considerations, to lift us pygmies onto the backs of giants. The issue of bias in using a model is raised so as to help us be aware of some limits and advantages. We must expect that it has both, that there are trade-offs. We must be free to criticize the model, to improve it, to raise ourselves beyond and above it.

A second way in which this presentation takes an evaluative approach instead of a neutral one extends even to the use of the name "metaphysics." The name has been used in its root sense —not from but *about* Aristotle. There were a variety of topics about which Aristotle wrote: biology, astronomy, etc. One area of his writings were classified as "meta" (after) "ta physika" (the natural sciences). How others reacted to this area of writings and what they wrote on these or related topics form an entire "corpus" of writings called metaphysics. For example, Aquinas wrote a commentary on Aristole's metaphysics. Descartes took one of the central Aristotelian doctrines of substance and said some unusual things about two kinds of substance. Berkeley argued for the non-existence of material substance. Leibniz viewed all substance as living. Into the seventeenth and eighteenth centuries there was a fairly well established body of writings about a certain sort of subject matter, traceable in a connected way back to Aristotle, which was called metaphysics. This is the sense in which the term "metaphysics" was used in these pages.

There are alternative uses of the name metaphysics. To some, philosophy is a difficult and obscure subject. If philosophy is understood as difficult and obscure, then metaphysics is most easily understood as obscure and heavy. Perhaps it is even overly subtle or too abstract. Hence any groping, any expression of confusion, is called metaphysical. For some, what is said does not have to be illuminating; in fact it is metaphysical when it is unintelligible. In still another view, metaphysics is the study of the occult, the magical. The following graduated list of variants of the name "metaphysics" can be generated:

1. in contrast to the physical; what is immaterial, incorporeal.
2. as above or beyond the laws of nature; more than physical or natural; supersensible.
3. as surpassing what is ordinary or natural; extraordinary; transcendent; supernatural.

4. as fanciful; fantastic; imaginary.
5. as the occult, the magical.

The model of metaphysics used in these pages has only sense 1. The other senses are rejected or disregarded. It is well to keep this choice in mind as a possible source of objection.

The treatment here has not been simply expository either in the model used or in the name, that is as regards what was admitted as data for consideration. Thirdly, neither have the writings of the philosophers been treated in only an expository fashion, that is, as simply what was held. In addition to the viewpoint held, there was also frequently included the "why" or the arguments for a given position. The arguments included were sometimes for a specific point being made and in other instances for a general view that was held. In both cases the treatment differed from proclamation or simple exposition of viewpoint. If arguments are included, then there can also be counterarguments. The process does not stop. There are counters to the counter. It might be shown that a given argument does not make its point, or that it makes its point but the point does not apply to the theory attacked, or the theory can be revised to make it immune to the counterargument, etc. It becomes endless. In philosophy there are arguments and counters. There is no end to the replies; one is never at a loss for an alternative or response of some sort. To be logical, however, the arguments must be to the point at issue. There must also be movement from one point to another, for example, from premises to a conclusion. One way to identify a deductive argument is that the premises establish the conclusion conclusively. If the conclusion is established only probably, then the type of argument is called inductive. It is likewise considered inductive if we give good reasons for a conclusion, but there may also be good reasons for conflicting positions.

In these chapters we have seen that a deductive system of metaphysics has never been successfully constructed. Such a position would be one that from a given starting point every other part of the system is tightly and conclusively deduced. The inclusion of single deductive arguments in the course of the exposition of a metaphysical system is something different. To give good reasons for and to establish probable conclusions in the course of the exposition of a metaphysical system is again something different. To some degree such inductive arguments have been now and again indicated in the text. Over and above this, a special thesis of this work is that metaphysical systems have at their cores a special mode of argumentation: instead of being by way of derivable consequences, it rather looks to preliminaries, assumptions, or presuppositions. This approach, as Kant called it, is transcendental. Much has been said about this; more is coming. The point so far is that philosophy concerns logical argumentation. The quality of a philosophical approach is found in the quality of its logical argumentation. This characteristic separates philosophy from, for example, poetry. Though some poetry is visionary, some didactic, it has been excluded from these pages. Argumentation has been used as one of the criteria for choosing what was included in these pages. One of the observable features of argument in philosophy is its endlessness. As was said before, there are always counterarguments to other arguments. One, perhaps less noticeable, feature in philosophy is about the types of arguments. Presuppositional or transcendental arguments always look back to starting points and beginnings. Some try to redo foundations and consequently undercut and throw out the work of predecessors. The frustrating feeling is that we never get anywhere. To do philosophy metaphysically one must be comfortable with the effort constantly to challenge and revise foundations.

In addition to the difficulties that can arise from the approach used in these pages, there are also objections already made in the text about metaphysical arguments and systems. One caution is that the text has no complete list of objections; neither are those contained fully developed. Here, rather than repeat what has already been done, the intent is to look at some kinds of objections that are exemplified in the text. Four general headings will serve as convenient groupings to gather together and organize what is scattered through the text.

A first kind or type of objection is that of inconsistency. This charge against a metaphysical system would be that one part of the exposition is in conflict with some other part. When these opposed parts are brought together the system breaks apart within. The charge of inconsistency was used as an objection against, for example, Plato and his system in which reality was twofold. It is entirely possible that the conflict of elements in a system can be reconciled by the process of having one of the two conflicting elements dominate and the other give way. The conflict is then resolved, and there is no further inconsistency. The resolution of conflicts brings out the positive point that there is a need for consistency, internal harmony, or unity. This is one of the demands of making a view a system. Consequently, doing metaphysics is doing systematic philosophy. There is at least this much of a connection to logic that the view proposed must be internally consistent. Otherwise a first general sort of objection is that the view presented fails to be a system because it lacks unity.

A second general type of objection is the reverse of the first. The objection is that the view proposed is so consistent that it is absolutely stable. This would be a static approach, wherein the claim is made that the metaphysical system is so tightly and completely constructed that one and only one system is possible. This ideal of a total system implies or even explicitly maintains that nothing else need ever be considered or added. This type of viewpoint, though not carried out to the extreme mentioned here, could result from something like Aristotle's view that the world is stable, always the same, never changing. In other words, the system shares the characteristics of the world that it portrays. If the world is unchanging, stable, and there is no evolutionary process, then the system must incorporate these same characteristics. But if it is an open universe that is in a state of evolutionary development, and if those who come to know it are continually opening up new vistas, then a static, total, and complete metaphysical system is not possible. Further, the inquiring human is part of the system. But the inquiry changes the inquirer, and so in this way too the data about which the system is constructed are in process of change.

Another variant of the stable system view is that the system proposed has the characteristic of certainty and therefore it is complete and no revision is possible. Here the claim is that one and only one system is possible and the one proposed is this unique system. The counter to this view is that even if all the facts are in and all the information is known, it is not the case that one and only one system can be constructed about these facts. And if a unique system about a given set of data cannot be constructed, then it is not possible for a metaphysical system to be certain. One way to counter the claim of a unique, certain, stable system is with the "indeterminacy of translation."

The end result of this last line of thinking is that a stable, unique, certain, or final metaphysical system is objectionable. One reason for the failure of stable systems is that the data are changing, either because the world is in a state of evolutionary change, the world is open to ever new exploration, or a crucial part of the world, that is the human, is being changed during the course of the investigation. In each of these cases what goes into the system of metaphysics, the fund of information, is in the process of addition and change. A second reason for the failure of a stable system is that even if the fund of information about which the system is constructed is complete and therefore stable, even then a system is not unique, final, or least of all certain, because from that same set plural alternative systems can be constructed. Given the reliability of these objections, the positive outcome is that a metaphysical system must adopt a process view of the world; such a system must be open to incorporate even further developments and refinements; and such a system must be able to tolerate alternative systems.

A third general objection about metaphysical systems is that they cannot include "unknowables." What cannot be established in experience is not admissible. Any claim about what is hidden cannot be borne out and must be excluded from a metaphysical system. For example, this objection can perhaps be made about the doctrine of substance in Aristotle. If it is not appropriate about substance, it is one made by modern science about essence and form in Aristotle. Locke's doctrine is that substance is the unknown and unknowable substrate in which the experienced accidental characteristics inhere, much as pins in some undetectable pin cushion. The objection to such a doctrine arises from the fact that every response to the search for specification and information is given by way of qualities or characteristics that can be experienced. But none of these experienced qualities or characteristics are by definition that which underlies or supports them. Hence, no identification, picking out, or specification can ever be given of substance as substratum. All claims about such a kind of substance are then claims about an "I know not what."

One explanation about the Enlightenment period in the history of philosophy is that under the probing of skepticism which was influential during the sixteenth and seventeenth centuries the developing natural sciences gave up the quest for substance, essence, and form or formal cause. The sciences settled for a lesser form of knowledge that consisted of probable truths about appearances. This sort of knowledge was in the mode of functional explanation of the practical everyday workings of the world in which we live and was adequate for the purposes of daily life. This knowledge was not considered to be a set of necessary truths about the nature of reality, nor about the real natures of things, and especially not about a transcendent reality. Whatever the merits of this explanation, there is no denying that about the time of the development of Renaissance science the role of the empirical, the observable, and experience became dominant in human knowing. But along with this new emphasis it was common to express a skepticism about human knowing and, consequently, to look for limits as to how much and what kind of knowledge was possible. The investigation turns to the question of what is human knowing? and the preliminary to this question: what is a human? No answer to these questions will be attempted here, but these are among the most controversial issues in philosophy. The issue of skepticism will receive further consideration with Hume and his predecessors. In sum, the outcome of the objection against the inclusion of unobservables in a metaphysical system brings about the emphasis on experience or the empirical. And since the only experience admissible is human, then a metaphysical system cannot have as its focus the world as it is in itself unrelated to humans, nor can its focus be a transcendent reality such as God. Humans, rather than the world or God, are consequently at the center of any metaphysical system.

A fourth classification of general types of objections is relative to the human being and the notion of person. The objection is that a metaphysical system which is impersonal is a distortion or inadequate. If the treatment of reality is depersonalized to the extent of excluding all reference to humans and makes claims about reality that exclude the knower and the act of knowing from the known, then this is a distortion of the 'real' or of existence. Knowledge is not only about something, actual or supposed, but it is also an activity and has as subject a knower. The system of objects without the act or subject is not a total system of reality. In addition, since all claims are knowledge-claims, then there can be no claims about things in themselves as if nothing else, not even human knowing, is involved. Nor can a metaphysical system be adequate that treats everything, humans included, as an "it" or in the third person. Some say this impersonalization is true of the system of Aristotle. Such an objection can be put to use instructively insofar as it shows that depersonalized (humans excluded) or impersonalized (third person) metaphysical systems are unacceptable.

But, as another alternative, it is possible for the opposite extreme to occur. Namely, a first-person metaphysical system that is so highly personalized and subjective that it has no further application, validity, or understanding than for its creator is equally objectionable. In other words, a metaphysical system cannot be inner and private to the extent that it cannot also be understood, tested, and adopted by others. Excessive personalization can occur because the expression of the system is private, unintelligible, or inapplicable to anyone other than its founder. It can also be excessively personal in holding that the human person is not expressible or understandable to any other person. Such would be a claim to an unobservable in principle and is exemplified in the dualism of Descartes. It might also be claimed that teleology in any anthropomorphic sense is an example of excessive personalization. Such a position would be one that attributes consciousness and feeling to nature, clearly with regard to inanimate nature, and perhaps more controversially with regard to lower life forms like plants, etc. The expressions that the sun is appointed to shine during the day and the moon at night are literal falsifications of natural processes. The falsification is clearly seen by asking what the sun shining at night would be like, or, why it cannot be night without the moon. In these sorts of views the notion of person becomes so all-pervasive that there is nothing from which the characteristics of personhood are excluded.

In the text the suggestion was made that rather than the expressions "subjective" and "objective" it might be better to use the expression "intersubjective." "Subjective" is to indicate that humans in their knowing are central to whatever is systematized. This centrality is so intimate that the questioner is part of and both changes and is changed by the question. In this sense metaphysics is reflexive. "Inter" is prefixed to "subjective" to indicate that the system is to be not only available to all but also able to be understood by all humans. To be public, observable, and human is the sense of intersubjective intended. Understood in this sense "intersubjective" and "objective" become closely allied, if not identified.

Here it will be helpful to carry a consideration of the characteristic of "reflexiveness" one step further. We can apply it not to specific objections about individual parts or doctrines of metaphysics but in its most general sense, that is, as an objection to metaphysics as such. The phrase of Gilson that "philosophy always buries its undertakers" is graphic. The requirement of reflexiveness shows that anti-metaphysics which pretends to be about metaphysics is part of metaphysics. A total rejection of metaphysics is, so to speak, "swallowed up" and becomes a part of metaphysics. Such a view claims to be the most basic and total viewpoint and one that should be adopted. Though it starts as if it were outside of what it criticizes, yet these same criticisms are incorporated and become engulfed by and part of what is criticized. However, this does not always neutralize the force of the criticism made; rather, if the criticism is worthwhile and to the point, then it may help to reconstruct or redirect metaphysics.

In addition to the four general types of objections about metaphysics there is also the issue of skepticism. In particular a skepticism about knowledge, about what can be known, has been a focal opposition to metaphysical claims. A standard distinction is the separation of extreme from partial skepticism. Whether the extreme skeptic claims to know nothing or makes no claims about anything is not clear; the first version appears to be self-contradictory; the second is mute and unsaid. Extreme skepticism is a theoretical position seemingly without any advocates, for as Hume says, it is the paralysis of all life and action. Partial skepticism, the selection of various doubtable areas of the field of knowledge, is a very real position. If the area that is doubted or denied is metaphysics, then a frequently used strategy is to place epistemological limits on metaphysics. In other words, such a skeptic points out that there are limits beyond which our human knowing cannot go.

Although skepticism has always been a philosophical issue, it becomes more fully a part of philosophy perhaps with Descartes, or at least at that time. It is not that Descartes is a proponent of skepticism, but rather that he allows full range to the force of skeptical argumentation. In the first place there is methodic doubt. Descartes employs the daring tactic of incorporating the skeptical procedure and showing its limits by attempting to doubt everything that can be doubted. Of course Descartes believed he could recoup all he conceded to skepticism and set the course of knowledge on an unshakable foundation. Then, secondly, Descartes gave open expression of dissatisfaction with the prior history of conflicting philosophies and unresolved disputes. He believed this to be a standing scandal in philosophy. He attempted to begin again from the beginning. Alternatively, since it was the beginning that Descartes challenged, it might be clearer to say that he began further back than his predecessors. He found a source of their errors in assumptions they made that were not warranted. Most specially these assumptions were about the possibility and extent of knowledge. The point is not that Descartes was a skeptic, although there are those who argue that skepticism is the logical outcome of his procedures; rather, it is that with Descartes it becomes fashionable to be explicitly aware of the skeptical position and to assume that one must include justification of any claims to knowing.

The British tradition in philosophy has been critical of metaphysics and metaphysical claims as far back as Hobbes and Bacon. John Locke in his major philosophical work indicates that part of his intention is to discover the limits of knowing. He explicitly recognizes that not all is capable of being known, and he treats this limitation as one of the important parts of his philosophical exploration. No longer is the assumption on the side of knowing; instead, justification must be given for claims advanced.

## DAVID HUME

With David Hume the restrictions that are placed on human knowing become more explicit. Hume has already been mentioned as one of the leading influences on contemporary philosophy. The influence has been mainly critical and skeptical. Hume's famous statement about metaphysics instructs us to burn any metaphysics books because they are useless, in that they do not contain any abstract reasoning about quantity and number, or experimental reasoning about fact and existence. There is also a not-so-famous statement that he makes about learning the limits of human understanding in order to "cultivate true metaphysics with some care in order to destroy the false and adulterated." The two statements help keep in balance the treatment of Hume. To call him a skeptic with no further qualification is misleading. Some recent sources suggest that his skepticism is a literary device. He delivers a simple refutation of extreme skepticism. Nobody could consistently be a skeptic because what he did would refute what he asserted. The advice, not to do what I do but to do what I say, stresses saying over doing. In the case of the extreme skeptic Hume maintains that doing is primary over saying. One and the same person cannot say (assert, defend) skepticism because what he does (action, life) will contradict what he says. To propose or defend skepticism is inconsistent with the know-nothing claim of the theory of skepticism.

Other than the extreme skeptic there is also the partial skeptic, and it is his position that best describes Hume and his stand about "school metaphysics." Because of the limits and bounds to human knowing, Hume's skepticism extends to what transgresses these bounds. He can say of metaphysics on the one hand that it is sophistry and illusion, whereas on the other he can also talk of cultivating the true metaphysics. The basic message is to confine human reason to those things which are within reach. There are only two types of reasoning. There is, first of all, abstract reasoning, which delivers certainty because a denial is self-contradictory. This is found in relations of ideas which are discoverable by the operations of thought without going to what exists in the world. Such reasoning is a priori and is confined to matters of quantity and number. The only other kind of reasoning is about matters of fact and existence. In this case a denial never implies a contradiction because the contrary to a matter of fact is always possible. These are known a posteriori and cover the entire field of human experience, otherwise known as matters of fact. Following out this distinction, which is called "Hume's fork," we see that if a given point is about existence, then it is not certain because the opposite is always possible; if it is certain, it is not about existence, because a denial is self-contradictory. What Hume calls "sophistry and illusion" or the "false and adulterated" form of metaphysics is that which crosses and confuses these types of reasoning. Such a metaphysics claims to be both certain and about existence. All who know the nature and limits of human understanding will deny such claims. In this they will be skeptics.

A further skeptical device in Hume's philosophy is found in a criterion he uses to circumscribe the limits of meaningful discourse. The mental activities of humans are first of all "impressions," which are original and vivid experiences, and secondly "ideas," which are derived and faint. All our ideas are from impressions; there are no other sources. In cases of controversy, doubt, or confusion a way to solve the dispute is to ask for the impression from which the idea originates. Failure to be able to connect an idea to the impression from which it originates is a sure sign that one has transgressed the bounds of sense.

Among the important ways that Hume has been an influence on twentieth-century philosophy three have been set out in the text. First of all there is the matter of restrictions on human knowing. Hume reinforced a growing trend by setting out specific devices for this restriction. Secondly, Hume's "fork," though not the origin, is one of the clearer expositions of the analytic/synthetic distinction which to this day has been one of the basic dogmas of empiricism. It was this distinction which Kant challenged in his project to establish a scientific metaphysics. Thirdly, the attempt to set up a criterion by which meaningful discourse can be separated out from the meaningless has been an important project for a large number of twentieth-century philosophers. In particular the verification principle of Logical Positivism calls for and will receive special treatment. Hume's work was done in terms of mental imagery, and this version tends to the subjective and psychological because experience is treated as a perception of the mind. In contrast, the criterion becomes objective and logical when it is propositions that are to be explicable in terms of actual or possible experience. Experience is here interpreted in outer signs such as seeing, doing, etc.

## IMMANUEL KANT

The main lines of Kant's system have been explored in a previous chapter. He is reintroduced in this chapter on objections because no one has done more to change the character of the metaphysical enterprise. The change he crystalized is the formulation of the transcendental approach and the elimination of the transcendent approach to metaphysics. One of the points on which Kant agreed with Hume was that many had been careless about human knowing. There was need for a specification of the extent and limits of human knowing. Priority must be given to detailing the restrictions on knowledge before the metaphysical enterprise could be successfully carried out.

Kant, as well as Hume, held that it was necessary to distinguish the meaningful and the meaningless, sense and nonsense. Kant worked out such a distinction by contrasting reason, in a special Kantian sense, with sensibility and understanding which are meaningful. In sensibility, objects are given to us; it is the source of data, facts, the raw material of intuitions. Secondly, by the use of the understanding objects are thought. The understanding does not provide data but operates on it; here, the data of sensibility are brought under intellectual control of concepts. Finally, the study of reason and its unwarranted claims takes place in the Transcendental Dialectic section of the *Critique of Pure Reason*. This section contains and lists Kant's objections to previous ways of doing metaphysics. Basically, Kant argues to eliminate transcendent claims. Sometimes these claims are transposed into transcendental claims, and at other times he exposes their contradictions and impossibilities.

To generalize: Kant's basic argument is that there cannot be a transcendent metaphysics. The reason is that experience is of phenomena, of appearances. The categories do not apply any further than the limits of experience. Philosophy is not of things as they are in themselves. It is the malfunction of reason that continually moves us to apply, unjustifiably, the categories beyond appearances to things in themselves. Transcendent metaphysics continually makes this unjustifiable move. The error is exposed by showing that its statements are incapable of theoretical justification. For Kant, to have theoretical justification means that a proposition must be proven to be certain so that the opposite is not acceptable. He does not eliminate transcendent metaphysics in one fell swoop by a single principle. His approach is detailed and individualized. He shows that for any transcendent claim there is either a substantial objection or the opposite is equally provable or contradictions arise.

To be more specific: Kant shows, for example in the case of space, substance, and cause (these are chosen because the topics have come up already in the text) that they are transcendental rather than transcendent. For example, "space" is not a thing in its own right nor a property of things in themselves; rather it is a necessary condition or presupposition of our having sense perceptions of a world of objects. We cannot say there is a world composed of "such and such" and "such and such" unless as a precondition the data are positioned and arranged in some way. Space is this precondition, or form of human perception, imposed by the mind on nonspatial reality; it is not an objective entity at all. For a second example of transcendental rather than a transcendent claim, "substance" is the way in which the appearances or the data of sensibility are brought under intellectual control. In this case the various appearances or outer faces are grouped together with a greater degree of permanence, arrangement, and unity than the sense impressions have. Without this grouping, which is an activity of the mind, the sense data would be chaotic and haphazard. This same sort of interpretation applies equally to "cause" and the other categories. Basically, the categories for Kant are forms of thought rather than modes of being. In this expression the transformation of transcendent claims into transcendental ones is clearly phrased.

Besides transposing transcendent claims into transcendental ones, Kant, in another part of his case against transcendent metaphysics, exposes the problems and difficulties that reason gets us into when it attempts to extend the categories beyond the field of appearances. The major portion of the Transcendental Dialectic is divided into three sections. The first section is the "paralogisms" which are sorts of invalid arguments relative to the transcendent doctrine of the self or soul. The second section is on the "antinomies" which are conflicting propositions, each of which is supported by conclusive arguments about a transcendent world or cosmos. The last section is about the "Ideal of Reason," in which the malfunction of reason is detailed as it attempts to take us beyond experience in its proofs for the existence of a transcendent being or God. For each of these sections there is an -ology: rational psychology, cosmology, natural theology. About each of these fields Kant is a negative critic of what is done by traditional metaphysics.

There is one other general point to be made about Kant as a critic of metaphysics. This can be done by setting out an explicit disagreement between Kant and Hume. Hume's fork shows us two types of propositions; the list is claimed to be complete. Kant's list is for three types; it is the third type, the synthetic a priori, that is unrecognized by Hume. Kant claims that this third type makes up the content of metaphysics rightly constructed. The validity of the synthetic a priori as a form of human knowing stakes out the conflict between the Kantians and the Humeans. Another way of stating the conflict is the legitimacy of the analytic/synthetic distinction as the cover for all knowledge. The synthetic a priori has been treated in a previous chapter. The reason for reintroducing the subject of the synthetic a priori is to bring out an additional point about Kant's doctrine which is crucial to his project. This point is the claimed deducibility of a system of synthetic a priori concepts. Such a system for Kant is the scientific system of metaphysics. When our knowledge is part of a system, then it is objective and certain. To know in the strong sense, which is worthy of being called metaphysical, is to be certain, so that the opposite is not worth consideration. Though this is not like Hume's relations of ideas, where the opposite is a contradiction, yet it is strong enough so that the merely probable is inferior and cannot be called knowing in the metaphysical sense. If we relax the notion of "knowledge" to include what there is good reason for, if "to know" means to get the best arguments even if only probable, then, contrary to Kant, we have room for a more tentative metaphysics. Such a metaphysics would not require certainty about individual doctrines, nor would it require a rigid, tight deductive system. A relaxation of these systematic requirements would allow for the obscurities and partial insights that are the source of the many conflicts and debates among the greats in the history of philosophy. It is not without reason that the most serious objections to the work of Kant on the subject of metaphysics are his rigid requirements. His list of categories which he takes from a table of logical judgments is considered by him to be complete and definitive; not one further nor one less is needed for a metaphysical system. The list is closed, finished, final for all times. An even more demanding requirement which he has great difficulty fulfilling is the deducibility of this system of concepts. In contrast, the proposal suggested here is to open up the list of categories to revision and addition; furthermore, once this is done, then the requirement of certainty and rigid deducibility no longer needs to be maintained. This approach accepts the negative part of Kant's critique which eliminates the transcendent or attempt to go beyond the limits of experience. It accepts the transcendental approach as being distinctive of philosophy and as setting it off from empirical science on the one hand and revealed religion on the other. It weakens the sense of "know" to relax the conception of systematic metaphysics, so as to leave it open to development and progress by way of future additions.

## RUDOLPH CARNAP

Many of the points that have been made in the course of this chapter on objections crystalize and come to a focus in the writings of a contemporary, Rudolph Carnap. He is interested in setting out restrictions on knowing because he is convinced that the history of philosophy is filled with examples of unwarranted claims to knowledge. He accepts Hume's fork. For Hume, the division was between relations of ideas and matters of fact; for Carnap, it is between tautologies and empirical statements. For both this is a definitive list of types of meaningful statements. Carnap thus joins with that part of the Kantian project that can be called the search for a criterion by which the meaningless can be separated from the meaningful. There is, however, a difference in that Carnap believes he has found a single principle which will do this work and have the general impact of justifying scientific language but rejecting metaphysics. Finally, Carnap has already been mentioned as one who, like Russell, focuses on language and its analysis rather than on private mental entities. Moreover, he, like Russell, engages in the work of constructing an ideal or formal language that will be free from the impurities and ambiguities of our daily language.

The treatment of Carnap here will emphasize the work on the criterion by which sense and nonsense may be distinguished. The criterion by which this was achieved is called the verification principle. In its main outlines the principle puts forward that there are two and only two classes of significant propositions. The one class consists of matters of fact, as Hume called them, and these can be tested by observation. The other class is tautologies, which are formal propositions about the meanings of the words or relations of their meanings; they are, so to speak, merely the rearrangement of symbols and do not make any statement about the world. Any other kind of proposition is not significant, not meaningful, does not make sense, or is nonsense. Strictly speaking, "verification" refers to a process that can be done about the first of the above two classes of propositions. Consequently, the principle of verifiability proposes that if a statement is to be considered meaningful it must be possible to imagine or conceive a state of affairs which would render the statement either true or false. The exact formulation of the principle creates many difficulties, perhaps as many as it was supposed to resolve. Sometimes the principle is specified in such a way that it excludes a large part of science; when it is broadened to include all of science, then the principle fails to exclude the sorts of statements that its proponents wished. For example, the process of verification could not be restricted to what was actually completed but had to be extended to the possible. Again, to restrict it to complete verification would exclude most scientific endeavor; so verification had to be extended to all that was partially verified. These were just some of the problems involved in attempting to get a satisfactory formulation of the principle. A second criticism is that the principle floundered because it was not itself verifiable. The proponents sometimes replied to this objection by claiming that the principle was not intended to be verified but was rather suggested as a norm. However, this response does not resolve the difficulty, because as a norm it is not binding on those who choose to ignore it. A variation on the second criticism takes us to the intended use to which the proponents and defenders of the verification principle wished to put it. Holding that there must be restrictions on knowledge claims, they tried to draw the line between the admissible and honorable pursuit of the empirical sciences as opposed to the unsettled disputes of metaphysics. The goal was to eliminate or reject completely the subject matter of metaphysics. The strategy, crudely put, was to find a principle that would show the empirical significance of scientific endeavor to distinguish it from what was not empirically significant; from the point of distinguishing it is then possible to slide from "not empirically significant" to "not significant" and end with "insignificant." Or, if one can distinguish the basis of science in sense observation from studies that were not rooted in sense observation, then one can slide from "not of the senses" to "non-sense" to "nonsense." It was the fixing of slogans such as "insignificant" or "nonsense" on the sentences of metaphysics that is so inflammatory to opponents of the verification principle. When cooler tempers prevailed, however, one response to the strategy of the proponents of the verification principle was to point out the nonverifiability of the principle and the consequence that it was metaphysical and to be judged also as "insignificant" and "nonsense." The technique was the reflexive one of turning the tables on an opponent by making his requirements apply also to his own work. If the principle was metaphysical, then it became a part of what was rejected. The counter-response of some less inflammatory Logical Positivists was to retrace their steps a bit and point out that they were developing a principle of empirical significance. Hence, there was nothing against the other studies being of some other sort of significance, for example, poetic significance, and such like. With cooler tempers prevailing it became the position of proponents of metaphysics to welcome the Logical Positivists as "brother" metaphysicians. This was for two reasons. First, as already stated, the principle of verification is now understood by all alike as being of the same type of discourse as metaphysical sentences. But secondly, from the generally agreed view that if a metaphysics proposes to give the most general view on the totality of "what is," then it must be that a Logical Positivist does exactly this, gives a total view on the nature of existence. True, it does not agree with other views, but it lays claim to the same bases that any other such view has. Philosophy in its metaphysical form has its ultimate revenge by incorporating its attempting destroyers. "Philosophy always buries its undertakers." Perhaps this is the last word on objections to metaphysics.

In closing, let us note a few special points about this last-treated sort of attack on metaphysics. The Logical Positivists differ from Kant, among other things, in that they were searching for a single principle to eliminate metaphysics whereas Kant considered piecemeal the various areas of transcendent metaphysics. Some have contrasted the two as the difference between the crudeness of the hatchet and the skill of the surgeon's scalpel. Of course, both have their uses.

Secondly, the Logical Positivists shared what has already been exposed as one of the limits in Russell's approach to philosophy. That limitation is the consideration of propositional language as if it were the only feature and function of language. All those sentences which are not statements about states of affairs or what can be true or false are disregarded. But language is much broader than propositional. Words have many uses and functions: questioning, giving orders, making requests, stating facts, describing, explaining, expressing wishes, telling stories, thanking, cursing, greeting, praying, etc.

However, the investigation of language conducted by Carnap, limited though it may be, has a focus that gives it great depth. An investigation of syntax becomes the explicit tool of the analysis of meaning. Carnap, as the heir to a direction pursued by Russell, is a particularly good representative of the trend to develop formal languages as powerful tools for the activity of philosophy. Syntax, or the rules of sentence formation, will make clear the elementary sentences from which all others are built. The primary sentences are called, by Carnap, "protocol" sentenses which refer to "the given" (whatever that may be). These protocol sentences are the basis of meaning, and their relation to other meaningful sentences is one of deducibility or reducibility depending on the direction in which one is going. Grammatical syntax alone is not sufficient to insure meaning to a sentence. Consequently, the structure of language, or syntax, needs further development. The task is to contruct a logical syntax of language which in great part consists of the rules for the formation of meaningful strings of words. Much of Carnap's life work has been in such books as *Philosophy and Logical Syntax, The Logical Syntax of Language, The Logical Structure of the World*, etc.

## MORRIS LAZEROWITZ

One of the points that the Logical Positivists attempt to make is that the metaphysical enterprise is not what it claims to be; while its sentences appear to be about existence and the real world in which we live, they are in reality pretenders or pseudo-sentences. The point made in response is that one who makes such an allegation is not different from what he is claiming about others. Rather than deny the point, the counter is to gather such a one into the same enterprise to which he is objecting. Much this same sort of objection and counterobjection is made by the last sort of theory that can be listed as an objection to metaphysics. Morris Lazerowitz, an American philosopher, has great admiration for the metaphysical theories that have been advanced throughout the course of the history of Western philosophy. He holds that the unusual feature of metaphysics is that the disputes among philosophers are never resolved, neither establishing a metaphysical theory nor refuting the opposition. It is this feature of interminable disputes that show all conventional estimations of the nature of metaphysical theories to be inadequate. Lazerowitz proposes a new theory about all metaphysical theories. Very simply, he psychoanalyzes metaphysicians. The outcome is to propose a three-layered structure to metaphysical theories. There is the conscious level of a theory about what exists or does not exist in the world. This level is a deception, because psychoanalysis shows that the rational conscious level is an illusion; it reveals merely the semblance of the world. Those who take the deliverances of metaphysicians literally are confounded and confused in their interpretations. To go a step deeper, the second or preconscious level shows that metaphysicians are proposing in their theories an alteration of language. What is happening in a metaphysical theory is a re-edition of the ordinary meanings of key words or expressions in our language. The metaphysician is proposing a revision in language of our views about the world. The third or deepest level is the explanation of these proposed revisions. The unconscious level shows that the metaphysician by means of his theory is letting out from his unconscious some repressed longings. His theory is to satisfy a wish or to counter a fear. The point being made is that metaphysical theories are pretenders and deceptive ones. They pose as being intellectual and rational. The explanation that undercuts this pretense shows that they serve the emotional needs of their proponents. Though Lazerowitz does not go any further, there are those who point out that the attempt to deal with "fundamentals" and get to the "bottom" of things comes from "cloacal" motives. Regardless of what it appears to be on the surface, it is, as Kenneth Burke would have it, a roundabout way of "making peace with the faeces."

The ultimate objection may then be to psychoanalyze metaphysicians and their motives by way of their theories. Of course, little expertise in reflexive thinking is needed to include Lazerowitz's analysis of the psyche within the frame of its own theory. It appears to be the ultimate depth approach to the nature of reality. But instead of dealing with the theories it rather uses the approach of undercutting the entire endeavor.

# VI
# PROJECTIONS

This, the final chapter, is both a summary and a survey. The intent is to bring together the positive points about metaphysics in general and, specifically, the viable characteristics of a metaphysical system. As a survey the chapter not only makes mention of what has happened but speculates on directions and developments that are happening.

Metaphysics is discussed by way of its characteristics. The characteristics should be general enough to be applicable to more than one metaphysical system, but specific enough to exclude some sorts of systems. The exclusion comes about by incorporating the objections of the preceding chapter. The generality should not be localized to any one system. The following example may make this point about generality clearer. Consider the three lines: 1., 2., 3.:

1. 7 pages × 11 pages = 11 pages × 7 pages
2. $7 \times 11 = 11 \times 7$
3. $a \times b = b \times a$

The lines become more general as they move from 1. through 2. to 3. As each line becomes more general the result is applicable to more cases. There is a sense in which 3. is more abstract than 2. or 1., and as more abstract and more general, it is more practical not less. Note, however, that in each line "×" signifies the mathematical operation of multiplication. It stays constant, and so does "=." If we construct a line 4. in which "m" signifies any of the mathematical operations of addition, subtraction, multiplication, or division, then the line which reads:

4. $a \; m \; b = b \; m \; a,$

which is still more general than the others, becomes sometimes true and sometimes false depending upon the mathematical operation signified by "m." Line 4. has no real use because its level of generality has gone beyond any useful distinguishing and discriminating. Further, if we construct a line 5. in which "y" signifies a mathematical or any other phrase whatsoever, then the line which reads:

5. $y = y$

is in one sense so general that it is applicable to anything and hence always true, or in another sense it is useless because it no longer conveys the sense of reversal of order that the original 1., 2., 3. showed. The point of the example is that the comments in this chapter should be general enough to be applicable to more than one metaphysical system, but not so general that they do not exclude any systems and then lose all worth and value.

One reason for the characteristics of metaphysics being general enough to apply to more than one system is the rejection of "finality." The feature of being final or being finished in a metaphysical system, though sometimes claimed, is now quite generally rejected. It can be claimed in several ways. It can mean that no other system is possible besides the one for which finality is claimed, that is, the system has the characteristic of uniqueness. Or it can mean that what a given system proposes cannot be false, namely, that it is certain. Or it can be that the system is complete and nothing more can be added. In whichever of these ways the claim to finality is put forward, it was considered and rejected in the previous chapter. As a consequence, any metaphysical system should be pluralistic in the sense of being able to tolerate alternative systems. It should also be open in the sense of being able to allow revision or substitution of important parts; this does not exclude the possibility that the revision could be so all-encompassing as to be rather the substitution of an entirely different system. The system should also be able to allow for additions by way of progress, which will give a system greater adequacy and completeness. In a word, the consequences of the rejection of "finality" are that a metaphysical system should be pluralistic, open, and admit progress.

Two of the major demands for systematic metaphysics are those of "unity" and "totality." "Unity," otherwise phrased as internal consistency, is the least controversial of the formal characteristics of a system of philosophy. It is a demand of logic, and the substantiated objection of inconsistency is one of the more embarrassing accusations that can be made. "Totality" or all-inclusiveness, as another formal characteristic of a metaphysical system, is in the fundamentals that are included and integrated. In other words, the totality is not empirical completeness of every single item classifiable as knowledge; rather, the completeness is of fundamentals with a wide enough sense of generality to cover by way of class headings or principles the specificness and range of individual details. The test of all-inclusiveness for a metaphysical system is the empirical applicability to the details of our experience. To find there are parts of human experience that are not covered, or that there are changes in experience that cannot be handled by a system, is to show a defect in totality. For example, in the ages before the invention of timepieces that permitted accurate time measure, the sense of the "present" or "now" was probably different. To say of a public means of transportation, whether it be a plane, bus, or stagecoach, that its arrival or departure time is "now" has a different sense when the traveler, driver, and dispatcher have accurate time-measuring devices in comparison to not having a measuring device. In the one case time is measured in hours and minutes, whereas in the other it might be as indefinite as days or weeks. The point is that the sense of time and the present moment or "now" must be adequate to cover vastly different specific situations. Any new situation that cannot be included under the basic concepts shows that some revision must be made so that the fundamentals are, in each case, included. As a result, the characteristic of "totality" which a metaphysical system must have looks, on the one hand, to basics or fundamentals and, on the other hand, to the specifics of experience.

In addition to being systematic, a metaphysical view must be primary. "Primary" is here treated as being both objective and basic. The sense of "objective" is neither impersonal at the one extreme, nor subjective at the other. It is not the study of a world of lifeless objects without the human personal element being part of it. Nor is it subjective in the sense of being so private and individual as to pertain to only one or be limited to only a few persons. Rather, objective here is understood as not only including but having at its center what is human and having it shared among all persons. It must be equally available to all, or almost all, on a wide enough scale of time and place so as not to come in and go out of style. Some might prefer to describe it as "inter-subjective." But "objective" is more than equally acceptable because of the stress it puts on universalization. A second way in which metaphysics is primary philosophy is that it is "basic." The "basics" are those truths which are sufficiently general to cover in an abstract way not only the essentials but also the specifics of our experience. "Basic" in one way gravitates toward the characteristic of "totality" already covered. The basics or fundamentals must be total or comprehensive. In yet another sense "basic" merges into a type of thinking, namely, reflexive thinking.

Reflexive is a special type of thinking appropriate for a large part of metaphysics. It fits with the previously mentioned characteristics. In one way it is a matter of consistency, the logical consistency of self-applicability. In another way it is so total and comprehensive that it is self-inclusive. Then again it is objective because equally applicable to all; itself is included, none excluded. Finally, it is related to basics which are to have a high enough level of generality to cover many specifics but not so high as to be harmless tautologies. Reflexive thinking is special to metaphysics as a study, namely, as an *objective* study of *basics* with *unity* and *totality*.

In addition to "reflexive" as a type of thinking, reflexive is a special sort of content and is a special mode of argument. It is called transcendental, or presuppositional, both in content and in mode of argument. It was Kant who brought this change into metaphysics. His critical theory took a new departure by defining the subject matter by the method of procedure. Other thinkers took for granted that the world could be studied as an object. True, it was special in that one gained access to it by "reflection" rather than by ordinary perception which yielded knowledge of external things. The notion of "world" even in pre-critical philosophy was not that it was just another object or totality of objects.

Transcendental philosophy is not reflection on objects or things; rather it is an analysis of the conditions of knowing and the results of such an analysis. Transcendental argument tries to infer from experience back to the subject of that experience. Its task is to uncover the necessary conditions of the experience that we have; what must we be like in order to have the kind of experience we do? Such an investigation reveals much about the nature of the subject which can never be found in the objects of experience. Kant, by proceeding in this way, was able to point out that the subject is never absent from the experience of the world or its objects; in addition, the subject is not exhausted by the phenomena given in introspection. Both in the observation of the self and in the observation of the world there is the underlying subject, who as observer is not the observed. The consequence is that "world" must be considered wide enough to include the self as observer with its activity and the dimension of an analysis of the subject. Such analyses can be performed only by a special sort of inference—that is, by arguing back from what experience is like to what the structure and contribution of the subject must be if this experience is to be possible. This sort of argument is called transcendental to distinguish it from both deduction and induction. These latter modes of argument are consecutive or consequential in deriving their conclusions from the premises. Transcendental arguments are connected to experience, but they work back to antecedents or preliminaries that are necessary; these are more frequently called assumptions or presuppositions.

The transcendental approach to philosophy is distinctive of metaphysics because here the concern is to probe the most basic elements of any sort of human experience. It is a new chapter in the history of philosophy; Kant called it a "Copernican" revolution. In one way the new approach broadened the scope of metaphysics because of the explicit and conscious inclusion of presuppositions; yet in another way it is limiting, because the human in the claims to knowledge is forevermore at the center and thereby included in any conception of a "world." In addition, the transcendental approach destroys the legitimacy of any talk about "things in themselves," or other possible worlds, or what is beyond human experience in this world. Kant showed by transcendental argument that the subject of experience has to be a unity; the unity is in the "I think" which must accompany all human experience. All claims about things as they are independent of the subject are baseless.

The world of experience is not ultimate reality for Kant; rather it is no more than the world of *human* reality. It takes its shape partly from the human subject, that is, from the structure of our minds. Transcendental argument is the way to explore these structures. Kant's revolutionary point was that because the structure of experience of the world is partly contributed by the knowing subject, then we must conclude that the shape of things as they are in themselves is forever excluded from consideration. The one nodding acknowledgement such things receive is that they must exist because the experiencing subject is *affected*, that is, our intuition receives its content from outside. But the nature of this reality, apart from its received status, is forever restricted from any further consideration.

It has already been suggested that Kant stopped halfway. He clearly saw the centrality of the human in the transcendental philosophical endeavor. But he located the focus of transcendental analysis in mental structures. The problem with mental structures is that they are ultimately left to what each one can say about himself, and only himself. Yet the structures which constitute the basic presuppositions of systematic metaphysics are to be necessary and universal. As mental they are inner, private, and personal. How they are to be objective, no less necessary and universal, is difficult to explain. This problem does not arise if our study is one about language, namely, if we make the transition to what was previously called "linguistic Kantianism."

To review briefly: First of all, to follow Kant, the study known as metaphysics is not of the structure of the world, that is the world as an independent entity free of humans. If there are any structures, they are of a world as perceived by a human consciousness. This would include humans and their knowing abilities, but concentrate its study on mental entities. The difficulty is that this approach turns out to be subjective, personal, private, or insufficiently distinguishable from what is subjective in an arbitrary sense. Consequently, and secondly, to go beyond Kant, the study known as metaphysics is not of the structure of our thought about the world but is of the structure of our language in which we talk about the world. This is a crucial change, and the greater part of the rest of the chapter is about the relation of language to metaphysics.

"Language" is here understood as a mass of expressions to which fixed rules are applicable, whether written or spoken. Two things are needed: meaningful expression and fixed formation rules. For the most part we are well enough convinced of the importance of language. Persons having no one to communicate with sometimes talk to themselves, or pets, or plants, etc. Among the more obvious ways in which language is important is in the communication of concepts. (Here, instead of using "idea," "concept" is a more neutral word in not having a commitment to the existence of private mental entities.) Words are public, substantial things or events and as such are specific and definite. Words can be used in gathering and expressing a body of knowledge which frequently is a collective undertaking. Results are achieved only in the cooperation of many workers over a period of time. Cooperation of many through the passage of time is achieved only by communication. And this communication is accomplished by signs, especially written and spoken words. What is perhaps less obvious but just as important is the way language is needed for the development of concepts. Words are more than a vehicle for concepts. The concept is elaborated and refined during the course of verbal production. In addition, the completeness and precision of a concept is achieved in the process of verbal expression. Such carrying phrases as "What I mean to say is . . . ," or ". . . in other words . . . ," are indicators not only of a second attempt to communicate, but also of a renewed effort to be clear to ourselves about what we say. A third way in which language is important is in the testing of concepts. A general scientific principle is that independent repetition by others is needed as a test of objectivity and validity. Here, the extension of the scientific principle is to the area of language. The test is twofold. First of all the accuracy and effectiveness of communication can be tested by language. The understanding of the other person, the grasping of what has been communicated, is tested by how well one can repeat, respond to, or put to use what has been said. But secondly, language is a test of the understanding of the first person; the words used are the test to oneself and others of whether one has really said what he meant and whether the claimed concepts are meaningful. The testing of concepts also shows how language can be dangerous. Language can conceal, because the words used may be an inadequate expression and may lead the hearer to misunderstand and be led astray. This helps to show the importance of testing for concepts. Insofar as this testing is accomplished by language, then it is not too difficult to adopt the strong thesis that, for all practical purposes, the words are the concept. The basic reason is that we can make no claim, which is justifiable, to anything more than the words.

If we can adopt the above position, to the effect that the test, the justification, of our concepts or conceptual activity is in the words or language that expresses it, *and* if we can conjoin to this a second premise that philosophical problems are not empirical questions but problems in the area of concepts or conceptual activity, *then* we have adopted a linguistic view of philosophy. Linguistic philosophy is the basic view that problems of philosophy are problems of language; such problems are treated and answered by reforming language or by understanding the working of the language we presently use. The shift in philosophy that has occurred is from talk about objects, past talk about ideas, to talk about words. The thesis maintained by linguistic philosophy is that the questions that philosophers talk about must be understood as questions about the use of expressions in language. The fundamental metaphysical endeavor is to uncover the presuppositions of such linguistic expressions. Not everyone has considered this thesis acceptable; it has been one of the main controversies in philosophy over the last quarter century. It is one of the major directions in philosophy today.

An advantage of adopting the procedures of linguistic philosophy as a method is that language is objective; it is a thing in the world and as such is equally available to all. The work of philosophy becomes understood as an approach to its problems by way of analyzing the meanings of words and analyzing the relations holding between words in natural languages. It is a public project in which all can participate. It makes cooperation possible and also provides a means of checking one by the other. Procedures can now be developed for reconciling disputes among the participants.

Mention has been made of natural language as the field for analysis. Since this is a choice which results from a decision about a controversy, it is worthwhile to be clear about the controversy. In the treatment of Russell it was mentioned that he was analyzing the structure of a perfect language. Such would be a language constructed to avoid the ambiguities and imprecision of a living language. The expressions of natural languages are often syntactically ambiguous. Though the ambiguity contributes to the beauty of the language and may give it value poetically, it more importantly detracts seriously from its precision and clarity. More explicitly, Carnap was seeking the logical structure of the world, and his attempt was to analyze the language of science only; all other modes of expression were grouped as noncognitive. Both Russell and Carnap argued that the cognitive part of language was what really counted because the aim or primary aim of language is to repeat and communicate factual information. They believed the justification for the importance and necessity of their task in creating an artificial language was in part because words in ordinary language are ambiguous; on this account, artificial symbols would serve better than words. Again, in being able to choose new symbols it was advantageous to use short symbols, even single letters rather than whole words; the consequence could be that in this way the sentences are shorter than ordinary language and substantially easier to understand. They also pointed out that the concepts required in science and logic are so abstract that new symbols are required because there are no suitable words for them in ordinary language. The clinching reason for their project was that the syntax of natural languages had too many exceptions and was not exact enough. Were one to retain the words of ordinary language and change the rules, then all the former associations remained and the danger of confusion resulted. Their conclusion from these reasons was that it is better to construct an artificial language with new words and syntactic rules of its own.

Impressive as this argumentation may appear, there are a few assumptions and key flaws. In the first place, this line of argumentation assumes that language has as its sole purpose the communication of facts. The question of truth or falsity arises each time a sentence is uttered; or, if it does not arise, then such a sentence is incidental and functions as a connector to keep the flow of factual information going. In response to such an assumption it is useful to point out the diverse uses of language: questioning, giving orders, making requests, stating facts, describing, explaining, expressing wishes, telling stories, thanking, cursing, greeting, praying, etc.

A second assumption is that of the limitation of focus or field of analysis to that of science. The assumption is that if science is not the only worthwhile field, then it is at least the main one; whatever else is worthwhile may be included, provided that the analyses cover adequately the field of scientific endeavor. The area of concern is more considerably limited when science is considered to be the natural sciences and principally physics or any other field in which logic and mathematics are the principal influences. The assumption that is being made can be challenged by the reminder that language has been around a lot longer and covers a lot more than the focus on scientific activity.

There are two more subtle but equally harmful assumptions. First, those involved in developing an artificial language assume that the elements of language, that is, words, sentences, etc., represent things independently of the actions or intentions of the speakers or hearers. They consider that it is the elements of language, not the actions or intentions of the speakers, that count in language. Such an attitude as this ignores language as connected intimately into the life and being of humans who use it. Then, again, there is the disregard of the purposes of ambiguity, whether it be part of stories, jokes, or simply the device used by humans to avoid responsibilities, etc.

The key flaw in the artificial language proposal is that we cannot reform ordinary language, that is, as long as reform is understood in the substantial sense of replacement by an artificial system and vocabulary. The point is that ordinary or colloquial language stands at rock bottom; it is not a tool that we use while developing another language. Any project to develop a specialized language must make use of what we now have as the point from which development must depart. The importance of this point is that any of the projects to develop an artificial and more technical language is not denied or refused, but is identified as being secondary and derivative of what is primary and basic, namely, ordinary language. The search for clarity and precision of expressions and sentences is a general problem which is equally relevant to specialized and technical languages. If communication is not achieved technically, then how else can it be done than by the attempt to reformulate in what alone remains common to all communicators, namely, ordinary language? This is what is meant by the expression, the "rock bottom" character of ordinary language. If the one and only task of language is cognitive, that is, to convey information, then doubling of meanings and inexactitude in syntax cause problems. But if to tell jokes, create poetry, pray, etc., are all part of language, then doubling and inexactitude are no argument against ordinary language. At best, ambiguity is an argument for creation of an artificial language to be used in those limited circumstances when the purposes and uses are limited to repeating or communicating factual information.

In addition to the limited argument for an artificial language which is secondary to our ordinary or colloquial language, an important point has been made in emphasizing the organic unity in language as a total system. It is in the later philosophy of Ludwig Wittgenstein that we find a more humanistic account of the language by which we live and think. It is a situational or organic conception of language. In this view language comes to life in the working connections of one part with another and in the situations of their use. There are families or clusters that go together; if the connections are broken they become perplexing or meaningless; life leaves them. The organic view of language gives a new emphasis in philosophy. It generates a language consciousness that is a new sort of self-consciousness. The human person and the humanness of the world are structured by linguistic forms. One's self and one's world are made and colored by the use and structure of language. Language as used here is not what the etymologist or grammarian treats of. It is used in a deeper sense which attempts to convey the power of language to dominate the realm in which humans are humans. It is the active role of language which gives style and form to what I as a human am in my being human. This view of language is of a form of life which modifies even the field of perception, not just the conscious conceptual structures.

The view presented here is not a new view, nor is it unique; but it is new in emphasis, and it is pursued nowadays with more self-consciousness than ever before. One older, closely related view was entitled "word magic." Under this phrase linguistics pointed out the power of language to create and order a world of diverse things. The application of language enables us to make familiar what is new, unique, or strange. The activities of naming, identifying, classifying, and categorizing are all ways of bringing what is so arranged within the sphere of the humanizing. The patterns of human action are related to the forms of language in action. Language is here viewed as the greatest and most refined of human actions. The definition of a human as a language-using animal who deals in symbols, in part captures this view. Humans create, use, and misuse symbols. Language not only distinguishes humans from other animals, but it also distinguishes various humans culturally and occupationally, for example, scientists, or artists, or religious people, or men of action. In this view the language of the scientist is the soul of the scientist, the language of poetry that of the poet, etc.

The notion of the self and self-consciousness is connected to language in a far closer way than was previously thought. It is constitutive of the self with its activities and practices. We will increase our sensitivity when we move from an ambiguous feel for the workings of language that we live by into watching and hearing it at work. Language is our form of life, and an awareness of the logic of language is transforming of self-consciousness. It is not investigation of the presuppositions of language in general but the language in which we talk about the world that is the area of metaphysical concern. The elaboration of what is presupposed by the way we talk about the world is simultaneously the elaboration of a metaphysical scheme and the development of a level of self-awareness. A self that lacks this sort of sense and sensitivity has by current standards not realized itself. It is not self-conscious to the fullest extent.

* * *

It should be possible to join together the characteristics of metaphysics in a single sentence; since the sentence is forced and awkward several samples are suggested. Metaphysics is a *unified* and *objective* view incorporating the *totality* of *basic* and *reflexive presuppositions* of our *language* in which we talk about the world. In this sample there are seven italicized key terms. The first part can be abbreviated by substituting "system" and "primary" for four of the characteristics: Metaphysics is a system of primary philosophy incorporating the reflexive presuppositions of our language in which we talk about the world. Another sample attempts to capture what has been done in these six chapters: Metaphysics is the study of the fundamental

| *presuppositions* | of some | *systems* of | *primary* | *philosophy*. |
|---|---|---|---|---|
| ↓ | | ↓ | ↓ | ↓ |
| reflexive | | unity | objective | linguistic |
| transcendental | | totality | basic | |

These last four italicized words are to be understood according to the words connected by arrows. Since there is not only one way to analyze presuppositions, several systems are possible and even several analyses of the same system. More than one system must be studied to study metaphysics.

# INDEX